我的爱情美文

最美不过初相见

英汉对照　词汇解析　语法讲解　励志语录

刘媛媛　编著

中国纺织出版社

图书在版编目（CIP）数据

我的爱情美文：最美不过初相见：英文 / 刘媛媛
编著. -- 北京：中国纺织出版社，2019.4
ISBN 978-7-5180-5092-5

Ⅰ.①我… Ⅱ.①刘… Ⅲ.①英语－语言读物②散文
集－世界 Ⅳ.① H319.4：Ⅰ

中国版本图书馆 CIP 数据核字（2018）第 119974 号

责任编辑：武洋洋　　责任校对：武凤余　　责任印制：储志伟

中国纺织出版社出版发行
地址：北京市朝阳区百子湾东里A407号楼　邮政编码：100124
销售电话：010—67004422　传真：010—87155801
http://www.c-textilep.com
E-mail:faxing@c-textilep.com
中国纺织出版社天猫旗舰店
官方微博http://www.weibo.com/2119887771
三河市延风印装有限公司印刷　各地新华书店经销
2019年4月第1版第1次印刷
开本：880×1230　1/32　印张：6
字数：200千字　定价：39.80元

前言

　　思想结晶改变人生命运，经典美文提高生活品位。曾几何时，一个字，触动你的心弦；一句话，让你泪流满面；一篇短文，让你重拾信心，勇敢面对生活给你的考验。这就是语言的魅力。通过阅读优美的英文短文，不仅能够扩大词汇量，掌握单词的用法，了解语法，学习地道的表达，更让你的心灵如沐春风，得到爱的呵护和情感的滋养。

　　岁月流转，经典永存。针对英语学习爱好者的需要，编者精心选取了难易适中的英语经典美文，为你提供一场丰富多彩的文学盛宴。本书采用中英文对照的形式，便于读者理解。每篇美文后都附有单词解析、语法知识点、经典名句三大版块，让你在欣赏完一篇美文后，还能扩充词汇量、巩固语法知识、斟酌文中好句，并感悟人生。在一篇篇不同题材风格的英语美文中，你总能找到引起你心灵共鸣的一篇。

　　读一本新书恰似坠入爱河，是场冒险。你得全身心地投入进去。翻开书页之时，从前言直至封底你或许都知之甚少。但谁又不是呢？字里行间的只言片语不总是正确的。

　　有时候你会发现，人们自我推销时是一种形象，等你在深入了解后，他们就完全变样了。有时故事的叙述流于表面，朴实的语言，平淡的情节，但阅读过半后，你却发觉这本书真是出乎意料的妙不可言，而这种感受只能靠自己去感悟！

　　阅读之乐，腹有诗书气自华；阅读之美，活水云影共天光。阅读可以放逐百年孤独，阅读可以触摸千年月光。阅读中有眼前的收获，阅读中也有诗和远方。

　　让我们静下心来感受英语美文的温度，在英语美文中仔细品味似曾相识的细腻情感，感悟生命和人性的力量。

编者

2018年6月

目录

01 The Measure of Love Is When You Love Without Measure
爱的限度就是无限度地去爱

Freda Bright says, "Only in **opera** do people die of love." It's true. You really can't love somebody to death. I've known people to die from no love, but I've never known anyone to be loved to death. We just can't love one another enough.

A heart-warming story tells of a woman who finally decided to ask her boss for a raise in salary. All day she felt **nervous** and **apprehensive**. Late in the afternoon she **summoned** the courage to approach her employer. To her delight, the boss agreed to a raise.

The woman arrived home that evening, finding a beautiful table set with best dishes. **Candles** were softly glowing. Her husband had come home early and prepared a **festive** meal. She wondered if someone from the office had **tipped** him off, or... why did he just somehow know that she would not get turned down?

She found him in the kitchen and told him the good news. They embraced and kissed, then sat down to the wonderful meal. Next to her **plate**

弗里达·布赖特说："只有在歌剧中，人们才会为爱而死。"千真万确。的确，你不会因为爱一个人而死。我知道有人因为缺乏爱而死，可我从来没有听说过谁因被爱而死。爱永远都不会多。

有一个感人的故事，讲的是有个女人终于决定去向老板提出加薪的要求。她一整天都焦虑不安。下午晚些时候，她鼓起勇气向老板提议。让她感到高兴的是，老板同意给她加薪。

当晚，女人回家后，发现漂亮的餐桌上已经摆满了丰盛的菜肴，烛光在轻轻地摇曳着。丈夫提早回家准备了一顿庆祝宴。她心想，会不会是办公室里有人向他通风报信了呢？不然他怎么知道她不会被拒绝？

她在厨房里找到了他，告诉了他这个好消息。他们拥抱亲吻，然后坐下来共享美餐。在她的盘子旁边，女人看到了一张字迹优美的便

the woman found a beautifully lettered note. It read: "Congratulations, darling! I knew you'd get the raise! These things will tell you how much I love you."

After the supper, her husband went into the kitchen to clean up. She noticed that a second card had fallen from his pocket. Picking it off the floor, she read: "Don't worry about not getting the raise! You deserve it anyway! These things will tell you how much I love you."

Someone has said that the measure of love is when you love without measure. What this man feels for his spouse is total acceptance and love, whether she succeeds or fails. His love celebrates her victories and **soothes** her **wounds**. He stands with her, no matter what life throws in their direction.

Upon receiving the Nobel Peace Prize, Mother Teresa said: "What can you do to promote world peace? Go home and love your family." And love your friends. Love them without measure.

条。上面写着："祝贺你，亲爱的！我就知道你会顺利加薪的。我为你做的这一切会告诉你，我有多么爱你。"

晚餐后，丈夫到厨房洗碗。她注意到又有张卡片从他口袋里掉了出来。她从地板上捡起卡片，念道："不要因为没有加薪而烦恼！你本该值得加薪！我为你做的这一切会告诉你，我有多么爱你。"

有人曾经说过，爱的限度就是无限度地去爱。不管妻子成功还是失败，这个男人都给予她完全的包容和爱。他的爱庆祝她的胜利，也抚平她的创伤。不管生活的道路上遇到什么，他们始终同舟共济。

特蕾莎修女在接受诺贝尔和平奖时说道："你能为促进世界和平做些什么呢？回家爱你的家人吧。"还要爱你的朋友，毫无限度地爱他们。

单词解析 *Word Analysis*

opera ['ɑːprə] *n.* 歌剧；歌剧艺术，歌剧业

例 He was also learned in classical music with a great love of opera.

他还是个酷爱歌剧的古典音乐家。

nervous ['nɜːrvəs] *adj.* 神经质的；紧张不安的；焦虑的

例 She was apparently a very nervous woman, and that affected her career.
她显然是一个很神经质的女人，这一点影响了她的事业。

apprehensive [ˌæprɪˈhɛnsɪv] *adj.* 忧虑的；惶惑的；有理解力的

例 People are still terribly apprehensive about the future.
人们对于将来仍然非常担心。

summon ['sʌmən] *v.* 传唤，召唤；鼓起（勇气）；传讯（出庭）

例 Howe summoned a doctor and hurried over.
豪叫了医生，然后匆忙赶了过来。

candle ['kændl] *n.* 蜡烛；烛光；蜡烛状物 *v.* 对光检查

例 The bedroom was lit by a single candle.
卧室里只点了一支蜡烛。

festive ['fɛstɪv] *adj.* 喜庆的；欢乐的；节日的，过节似的

例 The factory was due to shut for the festive period.
节日期间工厂将关门。

tip [tɪp] *n.* 小费；小窍门；末梢 *v.* 给小费；倾斜，翻倒；装顶端

例 The sleeves covered his hands to the tips of his fingers.
袖子遮住了他的手，一直盖到指尖。

plate [plet] *n.* 盘子，盆；金属板；底片，感光底片 *v.* 镀；覆盖；电镀

例 The plate broke.
盘子打破了。

sooth [suːθ] *n.* 真实 *adj.* 抚慰的；真实的；温柔的；甜蜜的

例 Soothly to say, I got up late.
说实话，我起来晚了。

wound [wund] *n.* 伤口；创伤；伤害 *v.* 伤；伤害

例 The wound is healing nicely.
伤口愈合得很好。

语法知识点 *Grammar Points*

① Freda Bright says, "Only in opera do people die of love."

这个句子中有一个结构"Only...do..."，是一个倒装结构，表示"只有……才会……"，强调opera。

例 Only in this way can the experiment succeed.
　　唯有这样做，试验才能成功。

② I've known people to die from no love, but I've never known anyone to be loved to death.

这个句子中有一个结构"die from"，表示"死于……"，相当于die of。

例 The old man died from cancer.
　　那位老人死于癌症。

③ Late in the afternoon she summoned the courage to approach her employer.

这个句子中有一个结构"summon the courage to do sth."，表示"鼓起勇气做某事"，相当于gather the courage to do sth.。

例 It took me six months to summon (up) the courage to ask him out for a drink.
　　我用了半年时间才鼓起勇气邀请他出来喝一杯。

④ ...did he just somehow know that she would not get turned down?

这个句子中有一个结构"turn sb. down"，表示"拒绝……"。同义词还有refuse和reject。

例 Why did he turn me down?
　　他为什么拒绝了我？

⑤ Upon receiving the Nobel Peace Prize, Mother Teresa said: "What can you do to promote world peace? Go home and love your family."

这个句子中有一个结构"upon doing sth."，表示"一……就……"，相当于on doing sth.。

例 Upon seeing him, she ran to him happily.
　　一看到他，她就开心地跑了过去。

经典名句 *Famous Classics*

1. Take away love, and our earth is a tomb.
把爱拿走，我们的地球就变成了一座坟墓。

2. Once you really need love, you will find that it is waiting for you.
一旦你确实需要爱，你就会发现它正在等待着你。

3. The only great thing about marriage is the only love between two hearts of mutual loyalty.
婚姻唯一的伟大之处在于唯一的爱情——两颗心的互相忠实。

4. The most important thing in a person's life is to find themselves, and in the marriage is to be found.
人的一生中最重要的事是发现自己，而在婚姻中则是被人所发现。

5. It is universally acknowledged that you are indispensible to me.
全世界都知道你是我不可或缺的一个人。

读书笔记

02 She Left Her Shoes
爱的遗鞋

She left her shoes; she took everything else — her toothbrush, her clothes, and even that **stupid** little **silver** vase on the table we kept candy in, just **dumped** it out on the table and took the vase. The tiny apartment we shared seemed different now, her stuff was gone, and it wasn't much really, although now the room seemed like a **jigsaw** puzzle with a few pieces missing, incomplete. The closet seemed empty too; most of it was her stuff anyway. But there they were at the bottom, piled up like they usually were, every single one of them. Why did she leave her shoes? She couldn't have forgotten them, I knew too well that she took great pride in her shoe collection. But there they still were, right down to her favorite pair of **sandals**. They were black with a design etched into the wide band that stretched across the top of them, the soles scuffed and worn; a delicate imprint of where her toes rested was visible in the soft fabric.

It seemed funny to me, she walked out of my life without her shoes, was that irony, or was I thinking of

她把鞋子留在了这里，其他的统统都带走了，包括她的牙刷、她的衣服，甚至我们摆放在桌上装糖果的银色小瓶子。她直接把糖果倒在了桌上，然后把瓶子拿走了。这个二人世界的小蜗居看上去已经和以前大不一样了，虽然原本属于她的东西不是特别多，可都给搬得干干净净，这间房子现在就如同一幅残缺的拼图，不再完整。衣柜也变得空空如也，里面的东西大多都是她的。然而就在柜子的底层，也和往常一样堆积在那里，她的鞋子却留了下来，一只也不少。她为什么要把鞋子留下来呢？绝对不可能是忘了拿。我知道她向来很宝贝她收藏的鞋子。可是，这些鞋子真的就躺在那里，还包括那双黑色的凉鞋，她挚爱的凉鞋。这双鞋有着宽宽的鞋面，上面还镂刻有花纹，鞋底已经磨损破旧，她的脚趾印还依稀可见于鞋内软皮上。

这可真让我百思不得其解，她既然选择离开我，却又

something else? In a way I was glad they were still here — she would have to come back for them, right? I mean how could she go on with the rest of her life without her shoes? But she would never come back. I know she wouldn't; she would rather walk barefoot over glass than have to see me again. But Christ she left all of her shoes! All of them, every sneaker, boot and sandal, every high heel and clog, every **flip-flop**... What should I do? Should I leave them here, or bag them up and throw them in the trash? Should I look at them every morning when I get dressed and wonder why she left them? She knew it, she knew what she was doing. I can't throw them out for fear she may return for them someday. I can't be rid of myself of her completely with all her shoes still in my life, can't **dispose** of them or the person that walked in them.

A deep footprint on my heart, I can't sweep her shoes away for they've left. All I can do is staring at them and wondering, staring at their laces and **strapping** their buttons and tread. They still connect me to her though, in some distant bizarre way they do. I can remember the good times we had, what pair she was wearing at that moment in time. They are hers and no else's; she wore down the heels, and

不带走她的鞋？这是一种讽刺吗？还是我想歪了？从某种角度说，我又暗自高兴——鞋子既然被留了下来，那么她总有一天会回来拿的，对吗？我是说没了这些鞋子，她以后日子怎么过啊？可是，她不会再回来了。我知道她不会的，她宁愿光脚踩玻璃也不愿意回来再看见我的。可是，老天！她怎么就把鞋子给留下来了呢？所有的鞋，包括全部的球鞋、靴子、凉鞋、高跟鞋、木屐、人字拖……我该怎么办啊？任它们放在这儿，还是打包扔掉呢？我是不是每天打开衣柜就要看见它们，然后冥思苦想她留下鞋子的目的呢？她一定是有意这样做的，她很清楚自己在做什么。这些鞋子我不能扔，因为我怕有一天她会回来拿。她的鞋就这样留在我生命里，彻底摆脱对她的思念是不可能的，无论是鞋子还是它们的主人我都无法舍弃。

她的鞋子在我心中留下的深印实在难以抹去，我只能痴痴地看着她的鞋，看着那些鞋带，然后傻傻地把鞋扣系好。这些鞋子仍然将我和她联结在一起，虽然方式是那样滑稽可笑。我能记住和她在一起的快乐时光，她在哪时哪刻穿着

she scuffed their sides; it's her fragile footprint **imbedded** on the insole. I sat on the floor next to them and wondered how many places had she gone while wearing these shoes, how many miles she walked in them, and what pair was she wearing when she decided to leave me? I picked up a high heel she often wore and absently smelt it. It was not disgusting I thought. It was just the last **tangible** link I have to her; the last bit of reality I have of her. She left her shoes; she took everything else, except her shoes. They remain at the bottom of my closet, a shrine to her memory.

哪双鞋子。鞋子是她的，不是别人的。鞋跟磨短了，鞋边磨破了，鞋内是她纤纤的足印。我席地坐在她的鞋子旁边，想着她穿着这些鞋子到过多少地方？走了多少的路？她最后下定决心要离开我时穿的又是哪双鞋呢？我拿起一只她常穿的高跟鞋，心不在焉地嗅了一下，我一点也不觉得恶心，因为属于她而实实在在能让我拥有的就只剩这气息了，这也是除了回忆以外她留给我的最后一丝真实存在。她把鞋子遗留在这儿，其余一切都带走了。它们躺在衣柜的底层，那个属于她的回忆的神圣角落。

单词解析 Word Analysis

stupid ['stuːpɪd] *adj.* 愚蠢的；迟钝的；乏味的；眩晕的，昏迷不醒的 *n.* <口>傻子，笨蛋

例 I'll never do anything so stupid again.
我再也不会做这种傻事了。

silver ['sɪlvə(r)] *n.* 银，银器，银币

例 He and Helen celebrated their silver wedding last year.
他和海伦去年庆祝了他们的银婚。

dump [dʌmp] *v.* 倾倒；倾销；丢下；摆脱；突然跌倒或落下 *n.* 垃圾场；仓库；无秩序地累积

例 We dumped our bags at the nearby Grand Hotel and hurried towards the market.
我们把包扔在附近的格兰德酒店后就匆匆赶往集市。

jigsaw ['dʒɪgsɔː] *n.* 拼图

例 We've got a new jigsaw puzzle!
我们得到了一个新的七巧板。

sandal ['sændl] *n.* 凉鞋，草带鞋；[植]檀香木 *v.* 使穿上凉鞋

例 Constant use had fretted sandal strap to the breaking point.
凉鞋由于经常穿，鞋带快磨断了。

dispose [dɪ'spəʊz] *v.* 处理，布置，排列；处置；决定

例 Just fold up the nappy and dispose of it in the normal manner.
把尿布叠起来，像平常扔东西一样扔掉即可。

strap [stræp] *v.* 用带捆扎；用皮带抽打；拼命工作 *n.* 皮带；带子；磨刀皮带；鞭打

例 Nancy gripped the strap of her beach bag.
南希抓住了自己沙滩包的带子。

flip-flop ['flɪpˌflɑp] *n.* 后滚翻，噼啪（声）*adv.* 连续啪啪作响地 *v.* 使翻转；使……突然转变 *adj.* 后手翻的；突然改变的

例 He has been criticized for flip-flopping on several key issues.
他因为在几个关键问题上临场变卦而备受批评。

imbed [ɪm'bɛd] *v.* 栽种（花等），埋置，把……嵌入

例 The thorn was embedded in her thumb.
荆棘扎入她大拇指里了。

tangible ['tændʒəbəl] *adj.* 可触知的；确实的，真实的；实际的；[法]有形的 *n.* 有形资产；可触知的或具体的某事物

例 There should be some tangible evidence that the economy is starting to recover.
应该有明显迹象表明经济开始复苏了。

语法知识点 Grammar Points

① She couldn't have forgotten them, I knew too well that she took great pride in her shoe collection, but there they still were, right down to her favorite pair of sandals.

这个句子中有一个结构"take great pride in"，表示"为……而感到骄傲"。同义词组有be/feel proud of。

 She takes great pride in her children's success.

她为自己的孩子们取得的成功感到无比骄傲。

② All I can do is staring at them and wondering, staring at their laces and strapping their buttons and tread.

这个句子中有一个结构"stare at"，表示"盯着看"。一般表示"注视"的单词搭配的介词是at，如look at和glare at。句首All I can do是一个句子，来做后面is的主语。

 She stared at me, smiling.

她盯着我微微笑。

③ …she would rather walk barefoot over glass than have to see me again.

这个句子中有一个结构"would rather do sth. than do sth."，表示"宁愿……也不……"。同义词组还有prefer to (do) A rather than (do) B，宁愿选A也不选B。

 I would rather die than eat the food.

我宁死也不吃这些食物。

经典名句 Famous Classics

1. Sometimes affection is a shy flower that takes time to blossom.

有时爱情是朵含蓄的花，需要时间才会怒放。

2. It doesn't matter if you have a weakness.

有点缺点没关系。

3. Happiness is too simple, so it is easily broken.

快乐太单纯，所以容易破碎。

4. Life is not a drama; it is more cruel than a drama.
   生活不是话剧，它比话剧残酷得多。

5. Ignorance turned out to be the most ruthless revenge.
   无视才是最狠的报复。

读书笔记

03 Love and Time
爱和时间

Once upon a time, there was an **island** where all the feelings lived: Happiness, Sadness, Knowledge, and all of the others, including Love. One day it was **announced** to the feelings that the island would **sink**, so all of them **constructed** boats to leave, except for Love.

Love was the only one who stayed. Love wanted to **hold out** until the last possible moment.

When the island had almost sunk, Love decided to **ask for help**.

Richness was passing by Love in a grand boat. Love said, "Richness, can you take me with you?"

Richness answered, "No, I can't. There is a lot of gold and silver in my boat. There is no place here for you."

Love decided to ask Vanity who was also passing by in a beautiful **vessel**. "Vanity, please help me!"

"I can't help you, Love. You are all wet and might **damage** my boat," Vanity answered.

Sadness was close by so Love asked, "Sadness, let me go with you."

"Oh… Love, I am so sad that I need to be by myself!"

从前有一座岛，所有的情感都住在那里：幸福、悲伤、知识和所有其他的情感，爱也不例外。一天，所有的情感听说小岛即将沉没，因此纷纷建造小船离开，除了爱。

爱是唯一留下来的，它希望能坚持到最后一刻。

小岛即将沉没了，爱决定请求帮助。

富有驾着一艘大船从爱身边经过，爱说："富有，你能带上我吗？"

富有回答："不行，我的船上载满金银财宝，没有你的位置。"

虚荣坐在漂亮的小船中从爱身边驶过，爱说："虚荣，帮帮我！"

虚荣说："不行，你全身湿透，会弄脏我的船。"

悲伤的船靠近了，爱请求道："悲伤，请带我走吧。"

"哦……爱，我太难过了，想一个人待着。"

Happiness passed by Love, too, but she was so happy that she did not even hear when Love called her.

Suddenly, there was a voice, "Come, Love, I will take you." It was an elder. So **blessed** and overjoyed, Love even forgot to ask the elder where they were going. When they **arrived at** the dry land, the elder went her own way. **Realizing** how much she owed the elder, Love asked Knowledge, another elder, "Who helped me?"

"It was Time." Knowledge answered.

"Time?" asked Love, "But why did Time help me?"

Knowledge smiled with deep **wisdom** and answered, "Because only Time is **capable** of understanding how **valuable** Love is."

幸福也经过了爱的身边，但它太开心了，根本没听见爱在呼唤。

突然，一个声音喊道："来，爱，我带你走。"声音来自一位老者。爱太高兴了，甚至忘了问他们即将去往何方。当他们来到岸上，老者自己离开了，爱才意识到老者给了它多大的帮助。

于是，爱问另一位老者——知识："谁帮助了我？"

知识说："是时间。"

"时间？"爱问："但是时间为什么帮助我？"

知识睿智地微笑道："因为只有时间了解爱的价值。"

单词解析 Word Analysis

island ['aɪlənd] *n.* 岛，岛屿 *v.* 使孤立

例 The island is presently uninhabited.
这座岛屿目前无人居住。

announce [ə'naʊns] *v.* 宣布参加竞选；宣布；述说；声称；预告

例 He will announce tonight that he is resigning from office.
他将于今晚宣布辞职。

sink [sɪŋk] *v.* 淹没；下落；退去；使下沉；使下垂 *n.* 水池；洗涤槽；污水坑

例 The sink was full of dirty dishes.
水槽里堆满了脏碟子。

construct [kən'strʌkt] *v.* 构成；修建，建造；创立；[数]作图 *n.* 结构（物）；构想；概念

（例）Every citizen has the duty to construct his country.
每个公民都有建设祖国的责任。

hold out 伸出；拿出；呈现；抵抗

（例）I should have held out for a better deal.
我应该坚持要求更优厚的条件的。

ask for help 求援；求人；乞援；借光

（例）Did he come to ask for help?
他来请求帮助了吗？

vessel ['vɛsəl] *n.* 容器；船，飞船；血管

（例）The British navy boarded the vessel and towed it to New York.
英国海军登上船，把它拖到纽约。

damage ['dæmɪdʒ] *v.* 损害，毁坏 *n.* 损害，损毁；赔偿金

（例）He was vindicated in court and damages were awarded.
他在法庭上被证明无罪，并且获得了损害赔偿金。

blessed ['blesɪd] *adj.* 有福的；神圣的；无忧无虑的

（例）Both are blessed with uncommon ability to fix things.
两人在修理东西上都有一手绝活。

arrive at 到达；来到；达成；获得

（例）From the day you arrive at my house, you need not spend a single penny.
从你到我家那天起，你就一个子儿也不用花。

realize ['rɪə,laɪz] *v.* 实现；了解，意识到；（所担心的事）发生；以……价格卖出 *v.* 变卖，赚得

（例）The support systems to enable women to realize their potential at work are seriously inadequate.
使妇女在工作中发挥潜力的支持体系严重不足。

wisdom ['wɪzdəm] *n.* 智慧，明智；常识，好的判断力；知识，学问；古训

例 Many Lithuanians have expressed doubts about the wisdom of the decision.

很多立陶宛人对该决定是否明智表示了怀疑。

capable ['keɪpəbl] *adj.* 有能力的，能干的，能的

例 The idea that software is capable of any task is broadly true in theory.

认为软件能够处理任何任务的观念从理论上说基本是正确的。

valuable ['væljuəbəl,'væljə-] *adj.* 有价值的；贵重的，宝贵的；可评估的 *n.* 贵重物品，财宝

例 Many of our teachers also have valuable academic links with Heidelberg University.

我们很多老师也和海德堡大学保持着有益的学术联系。

语法知识点 *Grammar Points*

① **One day it was announced to the feelings that the island would sink, so all of them constructed boats to leave, except for Love.**

这个句子中有两个结构 "announce sth. to sb." 和 "except for"，分别表示 "将某事公告或宣布给某人" 以及 "除了……以外"。该句中it做形式主语，that后面才是it真正的主语the island would sink。

例 They announced their engagement to the family.

他们向家里宣布他们已经订婚了。

I will thank everyone except for her.

除了她，我感谢每一个人。

② **Love decided to ask Vanity who was also passing by in a beautiful vessel. "Vanity, please help me!"**

这个句子中有两个结构 "decide to do sth." 和 "pass by"，分别表示 "决定做某事" 和 "经过"。前者同义词组还有make a decision to do sth.。该句中who做定语从句修饰vanity，who后面用的过去进行时，表示过去那个时候虚荣正在划船从爱身旁经过。

She passed by and ignored me.
她走过去，完全没有注意到我。

③ Happiness passed by Love, too, but she was so happy that she did not even hear when Love called her.

这个句子中有一个结构"so...that..."，表示"如此……，以至于……"。

 Amanda was so happy that she forgot to say anything.
阿曼达如此高兴，以至于忘了说话。

④ Because only Time is capable of understanding how valuable Love is.

这个句子中有一个结构"be capable of"，表示"有能力干某事"。同义词组还有be able to do sth.和have the capability to do sth.。

经典名句 *Famous Classics*

1. Time is a bird forever on the wing.
   时间是一只永远在飞翔的鸟。

2. Time is a great judge, even in the fields of morals.
   时间是伟大的法官，即使在道德领域亦如此。

3. Time is a versatile performer. It flies, marches on, heals all wounds, runs out and will tell.
   时间是个多才多艺的表演者，它能飞，能大步前进，能治愈一切创伤，即使消逝，也能留下影响。

4. Time is money.
   时间就是金钱。

5. Time tames strongest grief.
   时间能冲淡巨大的悲伤。

04 The Love in That Summer
爱在那个夏天

She was fond of Strauss, KFC, and Brazil **Espresso**. Dressed in decent gray skirt suit, she was busy working in a **modernized** office. That was her life before meeting me. Ever since our dating all those have vanished.

It was in 1997 when I started my so-called "great business". She followed me **wholeheartedly**. That summer came early. Flowers dyed the town dazzlingly red. We stayed in the **outskirts**, in a small room of a **condo** known as an illegal structure of this city. Wind blew through all the four walls into the room, the temporary home of her and me.

In order to save money, we walked to our store downtown every day. Lunches were always simple like **doggie** food, worth no more than 1.5 yuan for each of us. We walked back home at the end of the day, so beat that all we wanted was collapse into bed. It seemed that we made it through one whole year this way.

Those days were bitter. Business was my **totem**; love was her belief. Both supported us from falling apart.

We walked home late one day. She

她喜欢听施特劳斯的乐曲，喜欢吃肯德基，喜欢喝巴西的浓咖啡，穿着得体的灰色套裙在现代化的写字楼里忙碌。那是她遇见我之前的生活。自从她与我约会之后，这一切便消失了。

那是在1997年，我开始了我所谓的"大事业"。她死心塌地跟着我，义无反顾。那个夏天来得很早，花儿染得城市一片彤红。我们住在市郊，那是一个属于该城非法公寓的小屋，四面透风。那是我俩暂时的家。

为了省钱，每天我们步行至市区的店铺。午饭总是像狗粮一样简单，每人不超过一块五毛钱。晚上再步行回来，疲惫不堪只想倒在床上好好休息一下。整整一年，我们都是这样熬过来的。

那是一段艰苦的日子。那时，事业是我的图腾，爱情是她的信仰。事业和爱情支撑着我们，让我们紧紧相连。

有一次，我们很晚才到家。她坐在床边用水桶泡脚，

sat at the bed edge, washing her feet in a bucket on the floor. I went to the **landlord** for boiled water to make instant noodles. When I got back carrying a **thermos bottle**, she had fallen back into the bed, sound asleep, feet in water. She must had been extremely exhausted. One of her hands was under her body. I heard her light snore. I **tiptoed** to the bed and tried to flip her over so that she would be in a more comfortable position. I stared at her face, which was a young and pretty one and yet so wearied and exhausted. I saw one **mosquito** on this pretty face.

That summer my city was like a huge **steamer** box. We **put off** one day to another plan to buy a mosquito net, just to save money. I knew mosquitoes were flying all about in our room, but I seemed not to be bothered. So exhausted when I got back each day, I doubted if I would wake up even though someone cut a piece of flesh off my body, let alone mosquito bites.

That mosquito stayed at her forehead, sipping her blood greedily. She was still sound asleep, not feeling anything. Perhaps she was in a sweet dream in which our business was turning better. There came an abrupt **throb** of my heart. I reached to wave my hand at the mosquito. But it was not at all scared. I wanted to bat it to death.

我去房东那里讨开水泡面。当我提着暖水瓶回来时，发现她已经躺倒在床上睡得很香，双脚仍在水里泡着。她一定是累坏了，一只手还压在身子底下。我听见了她轻微的鼾声。我蹑手蹑脚地走到床边，想给她翻下身，好让她睡得更舒服点。我盯着她年轻美丽却疲惫不堪的脸，在这张精致的脸上，我发现了一只蚊子。

那个夏天，我所在的城市像个巨大的蒸笼。我们把买蚊帐的计划一拖再拖，只是为了省钱。我知道屋里蚊子到处乱飞，可我似乎并未受其干扰。每天回来后拖着那样劳累的身体睡下，别说是蚊子，就算有人从我身上切下一块肉，我都怀疑自己能不能醒来。

蚊子落在她的额头，贪婪地吸食着她的血。她依然睡得很香，毫无察觉。也许她正做着梦，梦见我们的生意有起色了。我的心猛地抽搐了一下。我伸出手驱赶蚊子，但蚊子对我的恐吓毫不理睬。我想用手拍死它，手扬起来，却不忍落下。我怕惊醒了她，她是真累坏了。我与她之间，有一只弱小的蚊子，此时此刻正叮咬着她。我僵在那里，手举在空中，可不知该做些什么，内

I raised my hand up high, but it could not descend— I was afraid of waking her up, she was really worn out. There lay a weak mosquito between her and me, doing harm to her right now. I froze there, hand in the air. I did not know what to do. I was worried. Suddenly, I began to get deeply **fed up with** myself. I hated myself. On the night of that summer, I stood by her side, feeling extremely guilty of her, of our love. The mosquito finally flew away. I forgave it, but I could never forgive myself.

In the daytime I went by a **peddler**'s stall and saw a pink mosquito net priced 16 yuan. That amount could be spent on a lot of other things. I headed back home without buying it. After she fell asleep, I got out of bed, stood by her side, and waved away mosquitoes with a hard paper board as a weapon. I was her temporary mosquito net all that night through. After a while she woke up to find what I was doing. She gazed at me, and ten seconds later tears flooded her face.

The next day saw a pink mosquito net in my room. We were both silent working together to fix it on our bed. In my mind I had presented the net as a gift to her. But I did not tell her that it was a gift. I was feeling that it was like a rose in full bloom. It was my **compensation** to love. Then I realized

心焦虑着。突然间，我觉得受够了，受够了这样的自己。我恨自己。那个夏天的夜晚，我站在她身旁，感到内疚，对她的爱极度羞愧。蚊子最后飞走了，我原谅了蚊子，却永远不能原谅我自己。

白天我经过一个小摊，注意到一个粉色的蚊帐，标价16元。16元在当时可以做许多事。我回了家，但却没有买它。那天在她睡着后，我起床站在她身旁，把一个硬纸板当作武器一样挥动着，不让蚊虫靠近她的身体。那整晚，我便是她的临时蚊帐。后来她醒了，看到我的行为，盯着我，10秒钟后，泪流满面。

第二天小屋里挂上了粉色的蚊帐。一起挂蚊帐时，我们都保持着沉默。在我心里，我是把蚊帐当成礼物送给她的，但我没这样说。我觉得那像一朵盛开的玫瑰，就算是我对爱情的补偿。但后来我意识到，其实什么也补偿不了她的爱。而那天恰巧是她的生日。

多年过去了，我赚了16万，或者确切地说是我们赚了16万。我们买了很多东西，却没有再买一床蚊帐。我们已经不再需要蚊帐了，住在精装的公寓里，已经飞不进任何一只

that nothing could really make it up. It was her birthday that day.

Years went by. I earned 160,000 yuan, or **precisely** we earned 160,000 yuan. We did a lot of shopping, but never a mosquito net anymore. We did not need any mosquito net, living in a very well decorated apartment, where no mosquitoes could fly inside. Nevertheless, I always feel that all my money, and all my belongings are far less important than the16-yuan mosquito net, which was invaluable to her, to our love.

蚊虫。可是我总觉得，我所有的钱、所有的这些东西，都远不如那个曾经只值16元的蚊帐重要。那对她、对我们的爱都是无价之宝。

单词解析 *Word Analysis*

espresso [e'spresoʊ] *n.* 浓咖啡，蒸馏咖啡

例 She orders a green tea, and I choose espresso.
她点了绿茶，我点了黑咖啡。

modernized ['mɒdə(:)naɪzd] *adj.* 现代化的

例 She lived in a modernized hotel.
她住在一家十分现代化风格的酒店。

wholeheartedly [ˌhoʊl'hɑːtɪdlɪ] *adv.* 竭诚地；全心全意地，全神贯注地；真心诚意地

例 I can endorse their opinions wholeheartedly.
我全力支持他们的意见。

outskirts ['aʊtskɜːrts] *n.* 郊外；边缘；市郊，郊区；从外围经过

例 We bivouacked on the outskirts of the city.
我们在市郊露营。

condo ['kɑːndoʊ] *n.* <口>各户有独立产权的公寓（大楼）

例 I remember my first condo.
我记得我第一个公寓。

doggie ['dɔgi,'dɑgi] *n.* 小狗，狗，汪汪

例 That's the place where I lived with my doggie.
那就是我和我的小狗住的地方。

totem ['toʊtəm] *n.* 图腾；图腾形象；崇拜物

例 This opera is one of the cultural totems of Western civilization.
这部歌剧是西方文明的文化标志物之一。

landlord ['lændlɔːrd] *n.* 房东

例 My landlord charges me for 500 yuan per month.
我的房东每个月收我500元的房租。

thermos bottle ['θəːrməs'bɑtl] *n.* 暖瓶；暖水瓶

例 I bought a new thermos bottle yesterday.
我昨天买了一个新的热水壶。

tiptoe ['tɪptoʊ] *v.* 踮着脚走，蹑手蹑脚地走；转弯抹角地谈论

例 He tiptoed out of the ward.
他蹑着脚走出病房。

mosquito [məˈskiːtoʊ] *n.* 蚊子

例 Mosquito is one kind of pests.
蚊子是害虫的一种。

steamer ['stimɚ] *n.* 蒸锅；汽船，轮船；蒸汽机

例 When does your steamer sail?
你们的轮船什么时候启航？

put off 延期；敷衍；使分心；脱去（衣、帽等）

例 My plane was put off.
我的航班延期了。

throb [θrɑːb] *n.* 脉搏；跳动，悸动 *vi.* 抽痛；（心脏、脉搏等）跳动

例 His head throbbed.
他的头阵阵作痛。

fed up with 受够了

例 I fed up with your disguise.
我受够了你对我撒谎。

peddler ['pɛdlɚ] *n.* 不法商贩，（尤指）毒贩

例 People laughed at the peddler's extravagant praise of his goods.
人们嘲笑这个小贩过度吹嘘他的商品。

compensation [ˌkɑːmpen'seɪʃn] *n.* 补偿，赔偿；修正；补救办法

例 He received one year's salary as compensation for loss of office.
他得到一年的工资作为失业补偿金。

precisely [prɪ'saɪsli] *adv.* 精确地；恰好地；严谨地，严格地；一丝不苟地

例 Children come to zoos precisely to see captive animals.
孩子们到动物园就是为了看圈养的动物。

语法知识点 *Grammar Points*

① **Dressed in decent gray skirt suit, she was busy working in a modernized office.**

这个句子中有一个结构 "be busy doing something"，表示"忙于做某事"。相当于be tied up with sth.。

例 Tony was busy doing his homework.
托尼正忙着做作业。

② **In order to save money, we walked to our store downtown every day.**

这个句子中有一个结构 "in order to"，表示"为了"。相当于to或者是so as to，但是so as to一般不放于句首。

例 In order to win, she practiced for 5 hours a day.
为了能赢，她一天练习五小时。

③ **She must have been extremely exhausted.**

这个句子中有一个结构 "must have been/done"，表示 "过去一定做了某事"。该句中exhausted表示extremely tired，极度疲劳。

例 He must have loved her because he did so much for her.
他曾经肯定是爱她的，为她做了那么多。

④ **So exhausted when I got back each day, I doubted if I would wake up even though someone cut a piece of flesh off my body, let alone mosquito bites.**

这个句子中有一个结构 "let alone"，表示 "更别提"。

例 I will eat all the things, let alone this piece of bread.
我会吃光所有东西，更别提这片小面包了。

⑤ **I was afraid of waking her up, she was really worn out.**

这个句子中有三个结构 "be afraid of" "wake somebody up" 和 "be worn out"，分别表示 "害怕做某事" "叫醒某人" 和 "疲乏，磨破"。of是介词，后面需要加-ing形式。

经典名句 Famous Classics

1. Where there is great love, there are always miracles.
哪里有真爱存在，哪里就有奇迹。

2. Love is like a butterfly. It goes where it pleases and it pleases where it goes.
爱情就像一只蝴蝶，它喜欢飞到哪里，就把欢乐带到哪里。

3. If I had a single flower for every time I think about you, I could walk forever in my garden.
假如每次想起你，我都会得到一朵鲜花，那么我将永远在花丛中徜徉。

4. Within you I lose myself, without you I find myself wanting to be lost again.
有了你，我迷失了自我。失去你，我多么希望自己再度迷失。

5. At the touch of love, everyone becomes a poet.
每一个沐浴在爱河中的人都是诗人。

05 Love Grew in Hearts
爱在心里成长

Maybe God wants us to meet a few wrong people before meeting the right one so that when we finally meet the right person, we will know how to be **grateful** for that gift.

When the door of happiness closes, another opens, but often we look so long at the closed door that we don't see the one which has been opened for us.

The best kind of friend is the kind you can sit on a **porch** and swing with, never saying a word, and then walk away feeling like it was the best conversation you've ever had.

It's true that we don't know what we've got until we lose it, but it's also true that we don't know what we've been missing until it arrives.

Giving someone all your love is never an **assurance** that they'll love you back! Don't expect love in return; just wait for it to grow in his heart but if it doesn't, be **content** it grows in yours.

Don't go for looks; they can deceive. Don't go for wealth; even that fades away. Go for someone who makes you smile because it takes only a smile to make a dark day seem bright. Find

或许是上帝的安排，在最终找到知音之前，我们总要遇到一些不尽如人意的人，只有这样，我们才能对知音这份礼物充满感激之情。

幸福之门关闭时，另一扇门就会打开。但我们经常只看见关闭的门，而对开启的门熟视无睹。

也许最好的朋友就是那些你坐在门廊下，看到的来回过往的行人。你与他们一言未语，走开时却感到那是你有过的最好的交谈。

无疑，一件东西只有失去后，我们才会懂得其真正的价值。可同样，一件东西在得到之前，我们并没有意识到它的缺少。

将爱全部付出，并不能确保一定会得到回报。别指望爱有什么回报，耐心地等待它在你所爱的人的心里生根发芽，成长壮大。即使不会，也要感到满足，相信爱已在自己心里成长。

不要追求华丽的外表，外表常常具有欺骗性。不要追求万贯家产，财富也会散尽。寻

the one that makes your heart smile.

找那个可以让你微笑的人，只有微笑才能让黑暗的日子变得光明。寻找那个能够让你的心灵微笑的人。

单词解析 *Word Analysis*

grateful ['greɪfəl] *adj.* 感激的，感谢的；令人愉快的；宜人的

例 You are doing me a great favor, and I'm very grateful to you.
你帮了我一个大忙，非常感激。

porch [pɔːrtʃ] *n.* 门廊；游廊，走廊

例 Is there a light in the porch or garden?
门廊或花园里有灯吗？

assurance [ə'ʃʊrəns] *n.* 保证，担保；（人寿）保险；信心，把握

例 He gave me assurance in black and white.
他给了我书面保证。

content ['kɑːntent] *n.* 内容；满足；（书等的）目录；容量 *adj.* 满足的，满意的；愿意的；心甘情愿的 *v.* 使满足，使满意

例 Empty the contents of the pan into the sieve.
将锅里的东西倒到筛子上。

语法知识点 *Grammar Points*

① **Maybe God wants us to meet a few wrong people before meeting the right one so that when we finally meet the right person, we will know how to be grateful for that gift.**

这句话中有三个结构 "want sb. to do sth."、"so that" 和 "be grateful for sth."，分别表示 "想要某人干某事"、"如此以至于" 和 "对……很感激"。be grateful to后面接某人，for接某物。

例 I want you to leave.
我想让你离开。

Please stand up so that everyone can see you.

请站起来，这样大家都能看到你。

I'm so grateful (to you) for all that you've done.

对于你为我做的一切，我很感激。

②**When the door of happiness closes, another opens, but often we look so long at the closed door that we don't see the one which has been opened for us.**

这个句子中when the door of happiness closes是一个时间状语从句，another opens是主句，but连接另一个句子。

例 When I reached the station, the train had left.

当我到达火车站时，火车已经开走了。

③**It's true that we don't know what we've got until we lose it, but it's also true that we don't know what we've been missing until it arrives.**

这个句子中有一个结构"It's true that"，表示"做……是真实的、准确的，或者就是这样的"。

例 It is true that the earth moves around the sun.

地球确实是围绕着太阳转的。

经典名句 *Famous Classics*

1. The only thing you can do when you no longer have something is not to forget.

当你不再拥有时，唯一可做的是令自己不要忘记。

2. I need him like I need the air to breathe.

我需要他，正如我需要呼吸空气。

3. I miss you not because of my loneliness but I do feel lonely when I miss you. Only when I miss you deeply I feel so lonely.

不是因为寂寞才想你，是因为想你才寂寞。孤独的感觉之所以如此之强烈，只是因为太想你。

4. If equal affection cannot be, let the more loving be me.

如果没有相等的爱，那就让我爱多一些吧。

06 Don't Let Scenery Always Be Far from You
别让风景总在前方

Once upon a time, a teacher and his student **lay down** under a big tree near a big grass area. Then suddenly the student asked the teacher.

"Teacher, I'm **confused**, how do we find our **soulmate**? Can you please help me?"

Silent for a few seconds, the teacher then answered, "Well, it's a pretty hard and an easy question."

The teacher continued, "Look that way, there is **a lot of** grass; why don't you walk there? Please don't walk backwards, just walk straight ahead. On your way, try to find a **blade** of beautiful grass and pick it up and then give it to me. But just one."

The student said "Well, OK then… wait for me…", and walked straight ahead to the grassy field.

A few minutes later the student came back.

The teacher asked, "Well, I don't see a beautiful blade of grass in your hand."

The student said, "On my **journey**, I found quite a few beautiful blade of grass, but I thought that I would find

很久以前，一位老师和一位学生躺在一棵大树下，旁边是无垠的草地。突然学生问了老师一个问题。

"老师，我很困惑，我想知道如何才能找到和我情投意合的伴侣。你能帮帮我吗？"

老师想了几秒钟，然后说："嗯，这是一个很难但又很简单的问题。"

老师继续说："往那边看，那边是无垠的草地。你何不过去走走，但是不要往回走，一直向前。当你走路的时候，试着寻找一棵美丽的草，然后把它拔下拿给我。但是只能拔一棵。"

学生说："那好吧……等着我……"，然后径直向草地走去。

几分钟后，学生回来了。

老师问道："我看你手上没有漂亮的草呀。"

学生回答说："我在路上发现了许多漂亮的草，但是我觉得我会找到更好的，所以就先没有拔。但我没有意识到自己已经走到了草地的尽头，你告诉我不要往回走，所以就一

a better one, so I didn't pick it. But I didn't realize that I was at the end of the field, and I hadn't picked any because you told me not to go back, so I didn't go back."

The teacher said, "That's what will happen in real life."

What is the message of this story?

In the story, grass is the people around you; the beautiful blade of grass is the people that attract you and the grassy field is time.

In looking for your soul mate, please don't always **compare** and hope that there will be a better one. By doing that, you'll waste your lifetime, cause remember "Time Never Goes Back".

棵也没有拔到。"

"这就是生活中经常发生的情况。"老师说。

这则小故事想要告诉我们什么道理呢？

故事里面的草地就是你周围的人，美丽的草就是吸引你的人，而草地就是你一生所拥有的时间。

在寻找人生伴侣的时候，请不要总是比较，希望将来会有更好的选择。如果这样做的话，你就会浪费一生的时间，请记住：时间一去不复返。

单词解析 *Word Analysis*

lay down 放下；规定；放弃；建造

例 The drug-traffickers have offered to lay down their arms.
毒贩们已同意放下武器。

confused [kən'fjuzd] *adj.* 糊涂的；迷乱的；混杂的；不清楚的

例 A survey showed people were confused about what they should eat to stay healthy.
一项调查表明，人们对该吃什么才能保持健康这个问题感到困惑。

soulmate [ˈsəulmeɪt] *n.* <口>性情相投的人，心心相印的伙伴（尤指异性伙伴）

例 If you find your soulmate, you should cherish him (her).
如果你找到了和你心心相印的人，你应该珍惜他（她）。

a lot of 诸多；许多的

例 I have lost a lot of weight.
我体重减了不少。

blade [bleɪd] *n.* 桨叶；刀片，剑；（壳、草等的）叶片；浮华少年

例 The blade of the oar had entangled itself with something in the water.
船桨的桨叶和水里的什么东西缠住了。

journey ['dʒɜːrnɪ] *n.* 旅行，旅程行期；历程，过程 *v.* 旅行，出游

例 There is an express service from Paris which completes the journey to Bordeaux in under 4 hours.
从巴黎有快车前往波尔多，全程不到4小时。

compare [kəm'per] *v.* 比较，对照；喻为；相比，匹敌；比较，区别；比拟（常与to连用）*n.* 比较

例 Compare the two illustrations in Fig 60.
比较图60中的两幅插图。

语法知识点 *Grammar Points*

① On your way, try to find a blade of beautiful grass and pick it up and then give it to me.

这个句子中有两个结构"on one's way"和"pick sth. up"，分别表示"在某人的路上"和"把……捡起来"，后者还表示偶然间学到某种语言或者技能。

例 On my way home, I came across a bunny.
在我回家的路上，我遇到了一只兔子。
I picked up French when I was in Paris.
我在巴黎的时候习得了法语。

② By doing that, you'll waste your lifetime…

这个句子中有一个结构"by doing sth."，表示"通过做某事……"。

例 By passing this exam, I can be enrolled by that university.
通过这个考试，我就能被那所大学录取。

经典名句 *Famous Classics*

1. Time never goes back.
   时间一去不复返。

2. Do you love life? Then do not squander time, for that's the stuff life is made of.
   你热爱生命吗？那么，别浪费时间，因为生命是由时间组成的。

3. Each moment in history is a fleeting time, precious and unique.
   历史巨轮飞转，分分秒秒的时间都十分宝贵，也独具意义。

4. Fish and visitors smell three days.
   鱼放三天发臭，客住三天讨嫌。

5. I am a slow walker, but I never walk backwards.
   我走得很慢，但是我从来不会后退。

读书笔记

07 The Late Letter of Love A
迟到的情书 A

I was always a little in **awe** of Great-aunt Stephina. Indeed, as children we were all frankly **terrified** of her. The fact that she did not live with the family, preferring her tiny **cottage** and being solitude to the comfortable but rather noisy household where we were brought up-added to the respectful fear in which she was held.

We used to take it in turn to carry small delicacies which my mother had made down from the big house to the little cottage where Aunt Stephina and an old colored maid spent their days. Old aunt Sanna would open the door to the rather frightened little messenger and would usher him or her into the dark living room, where the shutters were always closed to keep out the heat and the flies. There we would wait, in trembling but not altogether unpleasant.

She was a tiny little woman to inspire so much **veneration**. She was always dressed in black, and her dark clothes melted into the shadows of the living room and made her look smaller than ever. But you felt, the moment she entered, that something vital and strong

我对斯蒂菲娜老姑总是怀着敬畏之情。说实在话，我们几个孩子对她都怕得要命。她不和家人一块生活，宁愿住在她的小屋子里，而不愿住在舒舒服服、热热闹闹的家里——我们六个孩子都是在家里长大的——这更加重了我们对她的敬畏之情。

我们经常轮流着从我们住的大房子里带些母亲为她做的可口的食物到她和一名黑人女仆一块生活的那间小屋里去。桑娜阿姨总是为每一个上门来的怯生生的小使者打开房门，将他或她领进昏暗的客厅。那里的百叶窗长年关闭着，以防热气和苍蝇进去。我们总是在那里哆哆嗦嗦但又不是完全不高兴地等着斯蒂菲娜老姑出来。

难以想象一个像她那样身材纤细的女人居然能赢得我们如此的尊敬。她总是身穿黑色衣服，与客厅里的阴暗背景融成一体，将她的身材衬托得更加娇小。但她一进门，我们就感到有一种说不清道不明、充满活力和坚强的气息，尽管她

and somehow indestructible had come in with her, although she moved slowly, and her voice was sweet and soft.

She never embraced us. She would greet us and take our hot little hands in her own beautiful cool one, with blue veins standing out on the back of it, as though the white skin were almost too delicate to contain them.

Aunt Sanna would bring in dishes of sweet, sticky South African candy, or a great bowl of grapes or peaches, and Great-aunt Stephina would **converse** gravely about happenings on the farm, and, more rarely, of the outer world.

When we had finished our sweetmeats or fruit she would accompany us to the step, bidding us thank our mother for her gift and sending **quaint**, old-fashioned messages to her and our father. Then she would turn and enter the house, closing the door behind, so that it became once more a place of mystery.

As I grew older I found, rather to my surprise, that I had become genuinely fond of my aloof old Great-aunt. But to this day I did not know what strange impulse made me take George to see her and to tell her, before I had confided in another living soul, of our engagement. To my astonishment, she was delighted.

的步子慢悠悠的，声调甜美而温柔。

她从不拥抱我们，但总是和我们寒暄，将我们热乎乎的小手握在她那双秀美清爽的手里。她的手背上露出一些青筋，就像手上白嫩的皮肤细薄得遮不住它们似的。

桑娜阿姨每次都要端出几碟黏糊糊的南非糖果和一钵葡萄或桃子给我们吃。斯蒂菲娜老姑总是一本正经地说些农场里的事，偶尔也谈些外边世界发生的事。

待我们吃完糖果或水果，她总要将我们送到屋前的门廊，叮嘱我们要多谢母亲给她送食物，并要我们对父母转达一些稀奇古怪的老式祝愿，然后就转身回到屋里，随手关上大门，使那里再次成为一个神秘的世界。

让我感到吃惊的是，随着我逐渐长大，我开始打心眼里喜欢起我那位孤零零的老姑来。至今我仍不知道那是一种什么样的奇异动力，使我在还没有透露给别人之前就把乔治领去看望姑姑，告诉她我们已经订婚的消息。没想到，听到这个消息以后，她竟非常高兴。

"是英国人！"她惊讶地大声说道，"好极了，好极了。

"An Englishman." She exclaimed. "But that is splendid, splendid. And you," she turned to George, "you are making your home in this country? You do not intend to return to England just yet?"

She seemed relieved when she heard that George had bought a farm near our own farm and intended to settle in South Africa. She became quite **animated**, and chattered away to him.

After that I would often slip away to the little cottage by the mealie lands. Once she was somewhat disappointed on hearing that we had decided to wait for two years before getting married, but when she learned that my father and mother were both pleased with the match she seemed reassured.

Still, she often appeared anxious about my love affair, and would ask questions that seemed to me strange, almost as though she feared that something would happen to destroy my romance. But I was quite unprepared for her outburst when I mentioned that George thought of paying a lightning visit to England before we were married. "He must not do it." She cried. "Ina, you must not let him go. Promise me you will prevent him." She was trembling all over. I did what I could to console her, but she looked so tired and pale that I **persuaded** her to go to her

你，"她转向乔治，"你要在南非安家吗？你现在不打算回国吧？"

当她听说乔治已经在我们农场附近购置了一片农场并打算定居下来时，好像松了一口气。她兴致勃勃地和乔治攀谈起来。

从那以后，我常常到那所位于玉米地边的小屋里去。有一次，当斯蒂菲娜老姑听说我们决定再过两年才结婚时，她的脸上露出了失望的神色，但听说我的父母亲都对这门亲事满意时，她又放宽了心。

但她还是将我的婚姻大事经常挂在嘴边。她常常问一些怪怪的问题，几乎像担心我的婚事会告吹一样。但我没想到，当我提到乔治打算在婚前匆匆回一趟英国时，她突然变得非常激动。只见她浑身哆嗦着大声嚷道："他不能回去！爱娜！你不能放他走，你得答应我不放他走！"我尽力安慰她，但她还是显得萎靡不振。我只得劝她回屋休息，并答应第二天再去看她。

我第二天去看她时，她正坐在屋前的门廊上，流露出抑郁孤寂的神情。我第一次感到纳闷：以前怎么没有人娶她、照料和爱抚她呢？记得母亲曾

room and rest, promising to return the next day.

When I arrived I found her sitting on the step. She looked lonely and **pathetic**, and for the first time I wondered why no man had ever taken her and looked after her and loved her. Mother had told me that Great-aunt Stephan had been lovely as a young girl, and although no trace of that beauty remained, except perhaps in her brown eyes, yet she looked so small and appealing that any man, one felt, would have wanted to protect her. I came up to her. She hit the near chair with a light smile. "Sit down my dear." She said. "I have something to tell you."

经说过，斯蒂菲娜老姑以前曾是一个楚楚可爱的小姑娘。尽管除了她那褐色的眼睛尚能保留一点昔日的风韵之外，她的美貌早已荡然无存。但她看上去还是那样小巧玲珑、惹人爱怜，总能引起男人的惜香怜玉之情。我走到她的跟前。她拍着身边的椅子，淡淡一笑。"坐下吧，亲爱的，"她说，"我有话要告诉你。"

单词解析 Word Analysis

awe [ɔ] *n.* 敬畏；惊叹；惊惧 *v.* 使敬畏；使惊惧；使惊奇

例 She filled me with a sense of awe.
她让我心生敬畏。

terrified ['terɪfaɪd] *adj.* 很害怕的，极度惊慌的，吓坏了的 *v.* 使恐怖，使惊吓，恐吓（terrify的过去式和过去分词）

例 They could see that I was terrified, and hid me until the coast was clear.
他们能看出我很害怕，就把我藏起来，直到没有危险了才让我出来。

cottage ['kɑːtɪdʒ] *n.* 小屋，村舍；（农舍式的）小别墅

例 My wife and I have taken the cottage for a month.
我和妻子租下这套乡间小屋已经一个月了。

veneration [ˌvɛnəˈreʃən] *n.* 尊敬

例 This scripture has always been held in the greatest veneration in Mahayana countries.

这经文一直在大乘佛教国家受到最大的尊敬。

converse [kənˈvɜːrs] *v.* 交谈，谈话 *adj.* 相反的，逆的，颠倒的 *n.* 逆向；谈话，会谈；相反的事物；[逻辑]逆命题

例 They were conversing in German, their only common language.

他们正用德语交谈，这是他们唯一的共同语言。

quaint [kwent] *adj.* 古色古香的；少见的，古怪的；离奇有趣的；做得精巧的

例 The piano has a quaint old-world tone about it.

这架钢琴的音色具有一种古雅的老式风味。

animated [ˈænəˌmetɪd] *adj.* 活生生的，有生气的；活泼的，活跃的；愉快的；动画（片）的 *v.* 使……有生气（animate的过去式）

例 Everyone became more animated.

每个人都变得更加活泼热情。

persuade [pərˈsweɪd] *v.* 说服；劝说；使相信；使信服

例 They were eventually persuaded by the police to give themselves up.

最终他们被警方劝服，同意投案自首。

pathetic [pəˈθɛtɪk] *adj.* 令人同情的，可怜的；无价值的；荡气回肠

例 Don't be so pathetic.

别那么讨人厌。

语法知识点 *Grammar Points*

① **I was always a little in awe of Great-aunt Stephina. Indeed, as children we were all frankly terrified of her.**

这个句子中有两个结构"be in awe of"和"be terrified of"，分别表示"崇敬某人"和"害怕某人"。

例 I was terrified of my mother, specifically, in awe of her.
我很怕我妈妈，准确来说，很崇敬她。

② **The fact that she did not live with the family, preferring her tiny cottage and being solitude to the comfortable but rather noisy household where we were brought up-added to the respectful fear in which she was held.**

这句话里有三个结构"live with"、"prefer A to B"和"bring sb. up"，分别表示"和某人一起住"、"比起B更喜欢A"和"把某人抚养长大"。这个句子开头的the fact that引导了一个同位语从句，谓语动词是add，这一事实增加了我们对她的敬畏。

例 He lived with a famous poet last year.
他去年和一位有名的诗人住在一起。

I preferred English to maths.
比起数学，我更喜欢英语。

I was brought up by my aunt so I was not close to my mom.
我从小是阿姨带大的，所以和母亲感情并不亲密。

③ **As I grew older I found, rather to my surprise, that I had become genuinely fond of my aloof old Great-aunt.**

这句话中有一个结构"be fond of"，表示"喜欢"。相当于like、love、be interested in等。

例 I am fond of bunnies.
我喜欢小兔子。

④ **You do not intend to return to England just yet?**

这句话中有一个结构"intend to do"，表示"打算做某事"。相当于plan to do。

例 I didn't intend to teach all my life.
我并未打算一生教书。

⑤ **She looked lonely and pathetic, and for the first time I wondered why no man had ever taken her and looked after her and loved her.**

这句话中有一个结构"for the first time"，表示"第一次"。wonder后面引导一个宾语从句，表示为什么纳闷。

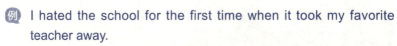 I hated the school for the first time when it took my favorite teacher away.

我第一次厌恶起了学校，因为它把我最喜欢的老师调走了。

经典名句 *Famous Classics*

1. Why do I always have tears in my eyes? Because I deeply love you.

   为什么我的眼里常含泪水？因为我对你爱得深沉。

2. I don't know if you'd like to be the one I love the most.

   不知道，你是否愿意做我最爱的那个人？

3. Whatever you do, remember to do it for yourself.

   无论做什么，记得是为自己而做。

4. Distance makes the hearts grow fonder.

   距离使两颗心靠得更近。

5. When a cigarette falls in love with a match, it is destined to be hurt.

   香烟爱上火柴，注定受到伤害。

读书笔记

08 The Late Letter of Love B
迟到的情书 B

She paused, as though she did not quite know how to begin.

Then she seemed to give herself, mentally, a little shake. "You must have wondered," she said, "why I was so upset at the thought of young George's going to England without you. I am an old woman, and perhaps I have the silly fancies of the old, but I should like to tell you my own love story, and then you can decide whether it is wise for your man to leave you before you are married."

"I was quite a young girl when I first met Richard Weston. He was an Englishman who **boarded** with the Van Rensburgs on the next farm, four or five miles from us. Richard was not strong. He had a weak chest, and the doctors had sent him to South Africa so that the dry air could cure him. He taught the Van Rensburgs' children, who were younger than I was, though we often played together. But he did this for pleasure and not because he needed money."

"We loved one another from the first moment we met, though we did not speak of our love until the evening of my eighteenth birthday. All our friends

她欲言又止，好像不知道从何说起似的。

接着，她仿佛振作了起来，说道："你一定想知道，为什么我听说乔治要回国却不带你走，心里感到非常不安。我是一个老婆子了，大概还怀着老人们的那颗痴心吧。不过，我想把自己的爱情故事讲给你听。这样你就能认清在你们结婚之前让你的未婚夫离开你，是不是一个明智之举。"

"我第一次遇见理查德·威斯顿时还是一个年轻姑娘。他是一个英国人，寄宿在离我家四五英里的一个农场上的范·伦斯堡家里。他身体不好，时常觉得胸闷气短。医生让他去南非，希望干燥的气候能治好他的病。他教伦斯堡的孩子们念书，尽管他们都比我小，但我们经常在一块玩。理查德是以教书为乐，并不是为了赚钱。"

"我和理查德是一见钟情，尽管直到我十八岁生日那天我们才彼此表示爱慕之情。那晚的舞会上，我们的亲友

and relatives had come to my party, and in the evening we danced on the big old carpet which we had laid down in the barn. Richard had come with the Van Rensburgs, and we danced together as often as we dared, which was not very often, for my father hated the Uitlanders. Indeed, for a time he had quarreled with my neighbor Van Rensburg for allowing Richard to board with him, but afterwards he got used to the idea, and was always polite to the Englishman, though he never liked him."

"That was the happiest birthday of my life, for while we were resting between dances Richard took me outside into the cool, moonlit night, and there, under the stars, he told me he loved me and asked me to marry him. Of course I promised I would, for I was too happy to think of what my parents would say, or indeed of anything except. Richard was not at our meeting place as he had arranged. I was disappointed but not alarmed, for so many things could happen to either of us to prevent us from keeping our tryst. I thought that next time we visited the Van Ransburgs, I should hear what had kept him and we could plan further meetings..."

"So when my father asked if I would drive with him to Driefontein I was delighted. But when we reached

都来了。我们在仓库里铺上一条宽大的旧毛毯，翩翩起舞。理查德是和范·伦斯堡一起来的，我和他壮起胆子共舞。但事实上，没有多少次，因为我的父亲很讨厌'洋人'。有一次，父亲曾抱怨说伦斯堡先生不应该让理查德寄住在他的家里，为此还跟他吵过一场，但后来就习以为常了。虽谈不上喜欢，但对这个英国人以礼相待。"

"那是我一生中最快乐的一个生日，因为理查德在跳舞的间歇将我领到外面清凉的月光中，在点点繁星之下对我倾诉爱慕之情，并向我求婚。我二话没说就答应了他的要求，因为我早已心醉神迷，想不到父母会说什么。我的心中除了理查德和他的爱情，什么也顾不上了。后来理查德没有来他安排好的约会处。失望之余，我没有大惊小怪，因为我们俩谁碰到形形色色的事都可能使我们无法幽会。我想等我去范·伦斯堡家看望他的时候，我就会明白理查德未能赴约的原因，再安排以后的约会……"

"所以，当父亲问我是否愿意和他一块开车去德里方丹时，我就高兴地答应了。但待

the **homestead** and were sitting on the step drinking our coffee, we heard that Richard had left quite suddenly and had gone back to England. His father had died, and now he was the heir and must go back to look after his estates."

"I do not remember very much more about that day, except that the sun seemed to have stopped shining and the country no longer looked beautiful and full of promise, but bleak and desolate as it sometimes does in winter or in times of drought. Late that afternoon, Jantje, the little Hottentot **herd boy**, came up to me and handed me a letter, which he said the English baas had left for me. It was the only love letter I ever received, but it turned all my **bitterness** and grief into a peacefulness which was the nearest I could get, then, to happiness. I knew Richard still loved me, and somehow, as long as I had his letter, I felt that we could never be really parted, even if he were in England and I had to remain on the farm. I have it yet, and though I am an old, tired woman, it still gives me hope and courage."

"It must have been a wonderful letter, Aunt Stephia." I said.

The old lady came back from her dreams of that far-off romance. "Perhaps," she said, **hesitating** a little, "perhaps, my dear, you would care to

我们赶到范·伦斯堡家，坐在屋前的门廊上喝咖啡时，却听说理查德已经不辞而别回英国去了。他的父亲死了，他是继承人，不得不回去料理遗产。"

"那天的事我记不大清楚了，只记得当时阳光惨淡，田野也失去了美丽的风采和欣欣向荣的景象，萧瑟凄凉得跟冬天或大旱时一样。那天傍晚，在我和父亲动身回家之前，霍但托特族的小牧童詹杰交给我一封信，他说是那位英国老爷留给我的。这可是我有生以来收到的唯一的情书！它将我的忧伤一扫而光，使我的心情变得平静——当时对我来说几乎类似幸福的平静。我知道理查德仍在爱着我。不知怎么回事，有了这封信，我便觉得我们不可能真正分开，哪怕他到了英国、我还留在南非的农场。这封信我至今仍保留着，尽管我已经年迈体衰，但它仍能带给我希望和勇气。"

"斯蒂菲娜老姑，那封信一定美极了吧。"我说。

老太太从她那久远的爱之梦中醒过神来。"也许，"她带着犹豫的神情说，"也许，亲爱的，你想看看那封信吧？"

"我很想看，斯蒂菲娜老姑。"我轻声说。

read it?"

"I should love to, Aunt Stephia." I said gently.

She rose at once and tripped into the house as eagerly as a young girl. When she came back she handed me a letter, faded and yellow with age, the edges of the envelope worn and frayed as though it had been much handled. But when I came to open it I found that the seal was unbroken.

"Open it, open it." said Great-aunt Stephia, and her voice was shaking.

I broke the seal and read.

It was not a love letter in the true sense of the word, but pages of the minutest directions of how "my sweetest Phina" was to elude her father's **vigilance**, creep down to the drift at night and there meet Jantje with a horse which would take her to Smitsdorp. There she was to go to "my true friend, Henry Wilson", who would give her money and make arrangements for her to follow her lover to Cape Town and from there to England, "where, my love, we can be married at once. But if, my dearest, you are not sure that you can face life with me in a land strange to you, then do not take this important step, for I love you too much to wish you the smallest unhappiness. If you do not come, and if I do not hear from you, then I shall know that you could never

她猛地站起身，奔进屋里，急切得像个小姑娘。她从屋里出来后，递给我一封信。由于天长日久，那信已经褪色发黄，信封边已经磨损，好像曾被摩挲过好多次。但在取信时，我发现封口还没有拆开。

"拆开，拆开吧！"斯蒂菲娜老姑声音颤抖地说。

我撕开封口，开始念信。

严格说来，它算不上是一封情书，实际上只是几页内容详尽的行动指南。信里讲了"我最亲爱的菲娜"该怎么摆脱她父亲的监视，夜里逃出家门，詹杰会在浅滩上牵马等着她，然后将她驮到史密斯多普，到了那里再去找理查德的"知心朋友亨利·威尔逊"，他会给她钱为她做好安排，使她能跟随她的情人到开普敦，随后转道英国。"亲爱的，这样我们就可以在英国结婚了。但是我的至爱，如果你不能保证你能在一个陌生的地方和我一块生活，你就不必采取这个重大行动，因为我太爱你了，不能让你感到丝毫不快。如果你不来，如果我收不到你的回信，我就会知道，让你离开你挚爱的亲人和乡土，你不会感到幸福。但如果你能兑现诺言却由于生性持重胆怯不愿单身

be happy so far from the people and the country which you love. If, however, you feel you can keep your promise to me, but are of too timid and modest a journey to England unaccompanied, then write to me, and I will, by some means, return to fetch my bride."

I read no further.

"But Aunt Phina!" I gasped. "Why... why...?"

The old lady was watching me with **trembling** eagerness, her face flushed and her eyes bright with expectation. "Read it aloud, my dear." she said. "I want to hear every word of it. There was never anyone I could trust... Uitlanders were hated in my young days... I could not ask anyone."

"But, Auntie, don't you even know what he wrote?"

The old lady looked down, troubled and shy like a child who has unwittingly done wrong.

"No, dear." she said, speaking very low. "You see, I never learned to read."

前往英国，就来信告诉我，那我就会设法回南非来迎接我的新娘。"

我没有再念下去。

"可是，菲娜老姑，"我气喘吁吁地说，"为什么……为什么……"

老太太的身子由于渴望知道信的内容而颤抖，她的眼睛炯炯有神地凝视着我，脸庞因急切的期待一片绯红。"亲爱的，大声念吧！"她说，"信里的一字一句，我都要听！当时我找不到可靠的人给我念……我年轻时，'洋人'是被人深恶痛绝的……我找不到人给我念啊！"

"可是老姑，难道你一直不知道信里的事吗？"

老太太低头俯视着，像一个无心做错事的孩子一样怯生生的。

"不知道，亲爱的，"她用低沉的声调说，"你知道，我从来没有念过书啊！"

单词解析 *Word Analysis*

board [bɔːrd] *n.* 板；董事会；甲板；膳食 *v.* 上（船、车或飞机）；收费供……膳宿；使搭伙，使寄宿

例 He wrote a few more notes on the board.
他在黑板上又写了几条注释。

homestead ['houmsted] *n.* 家宅，宅地；农场

例 A homestead cannot be the subject of a sale by court in order to satisfy the creditor.

宅地不能成为法院命令的满足债权人所要求的销售对象。

herd boy 牧童，牛郎

例 Late that afternoon, Jantje, the little Hottentot herd boy, came up to me and handed me a letter, which he said the English baas had left for me.

那天傍晚，霍但托特族的小牧童詹杰交给我一封信，他说是那位英国老爷留给我的。

bitterness ['bɪtənɪs] *n.* 苦味；痛苦；悲痛；酷烈

例 When he spoke, his voice was thick with bitterness.

他说话时，声音低沉，充满痛苦。

hesitate ['hezɪteɪt] *v.* 犹豫，踌躇；不愿；支吾；对……犹豫；不情愿

例 Some parents hesitate to take these steps because they suspect that their children are exaggerating.

一些家长不愿意采取这些措施，因为他们怀疑自己的孩子在夸大其词。

vigilance ['vɪdʒələns] *n.* 警惕；警戒；<正>警觉；<医>失眠症

例 Don't slacken your vigilance.

不要麻痹大意。

trembling ['trembəlɪŋ] *n.* 发抖 *adj.* 发抖的 *v.* 颤动；发抖（tremble的现在分词）；焦虑；轻轻摇晃

例 With trembling fingers, he removed the camera from his pocket.

他手指哆嗦着从口袋里取出相机。

语法知识点 Grammar Points

① **I am an old woman, and perhaps I have the silly fancies of the old, but I should like to tell you my own love story, and then you can decide whether it is wise for your man to leave you before you are married.**

本句涉及一个由whether引导的宾语从句，在宾语从句中，有一个it is+adj.+(for sb.)+to do sth.结构，这个结构中，it为形式主语，真正的主语是to引导的动词不定式。

例 It's very hard for him to study two languages.

对他来说学两门外语是很难的。

It is a little difficult for me to work out this question.

解出这道题对我来说有点难。

②**It was the only love letter I ever received, but it turned all my bitterness and grief into a peacefulness which was the nearest I could get, then, to happiness.**

本句结构较为复杂，I ever received是省略了that的定语从句，修饰love letter；which was the nearest I could get也是一个定语从句，修饰peacefulness。"turn into"意思是"成为，变成"。

例 It could well turn into some kind of a media circus.

这很可能会演变成媒体的一场闹剧。

The fighting is threatening to turn into full-scale war.

这场战斗有可能会演变为全面的战争。

③**Indeed, for a time he had quarreled with my neighbor Van Rensburg for allowing Richard to board with him, but afterwards he got used to the idea, and was always polite to the Englishman, though he never liked him.**

这个句子中有四个结构"quarrel with"、"allow sb. to do sth."、"get used to"和"be polite to"，分别表示"和某人争吵"、"允许某人做某事"、"习惯于"和"对……有礼貌"。allow后面若是不加sb.，就直接用allow doing sth.，表示允许做某事。

例 I quarreled with my mother because she didn't allow me to learn Japanese.

我和我妈大吵了一架，因为她不让我学日语。

You have to get used to that.

你得适应那个。

I am always polite to the teachers.

我对老师向来彬彬有礼。

④ **I was disappointed but not alarmed, for so many things could happen to either of us to prevent us from keeping our tryst.**

这个句子中有一个结构 "prevent sb. from doing sth."，表示 "阻碍某人干某事"，相当于stop sb. from doing sth.。

例 The boy's fear prevented him from trying.
男孩很担心，不敢尝试。

经典名句 *Famous Classics*

1. Ten men banded together in love can do what ten thousand separately would fail in.
同心协力的十个人能够完成一万个分散的人做不到的事情。

2. Love is a fruit in season at all times, and within the reach of every hand.
爱是一年四季每个人都能得到的果实。

3. Love is a master key which opens the gate of happiness.
爱是打开快乐之门的万能钥匙。

4. As selfishness and complaint cloud the mind, so love with its joy clears and sharpens the vision.
自私和抱怨使心灵阴暗，愉悦的爱则使视野明朗开阔。

5. The good life is one inspired by love and guided by knowledge.
美好的生活由爱所激励，由知识所指导。

读书笔记

09 When Love Beckons to You
当爱召唤你时

When love **beckons** to you, follow her, though her ways are hard and **steep**. And when her wings **enfold** you, **yield** to her, though the **sword** hidden among her pinions may wound you. And when she speaks to you, believe in her, though her voice may **shatter** your dreams as the north wind lays waste the garden.

For even as love crowns you so shall she **crucify** you. Even as she is for your growth so is she for your **pruning**. Even as she **ascends** to your height and caresses your tenderest branches that quiver in the sun, so shall she **descend** to your roots and shake them in their **clinging to** the earth.

But if, in your fear, you would **seek** only love's peace and love's pleasure, then it is better for you that you cover your **nakedness** and pass out of love's threshing-floor, into the season less world where you shall laugh, but not all of your laughter, and weep, but not all of your tears. Love gives **naught** but itself and takes naught but from itself. Love possesses not, nor would it be possessed, for love is sufficient unto love.

Love has no other desire but to fulfill itself. But if you love and must

当爱召唤你时，请追随她，尽管爱的道路艰难险峻。当爱的羽翼拥抱你时，请顺从她，尽管隐藏在其羽翼下的剑可能会伤到你。当爱向你诉说时，请相信她，尽管她的声音可能会打破你的梦想，就如同北风吹落花园里所有的花瓣。

爱会给你戴上桂冠，也会折磨你。爱会助你成长，也会给你修枝。爱会上升到枝头，抚爱你在阳光下颤动的嫩枝，也会下潜至根部，撼动你紧抓泥土的根基。

但是，如果你在恐惧中只想寻求爱的平和与快乐，那你就最好掩盖住真实的自我，避开爱的考验，进入不分季节的世界，在那里你将欢笑，但并不是开怀大笑；你将哭泣，但并非尽情地哭。爱只将自己付出，也只得到自己。爱一无所有，也不会为谁所有，因为爱本身就已自足。

爱除了实现自我别无他求。但是如果你爱而又有所求，那就请期望：

将自己融化并像奔流的溪

have **desires**, let these be your desires:

To melt and be like a running brook that sings its **melody** to the night.

To know the pain of too much tenderness.

To be wounded by your own understandings of love willingly and joyfully.

To wake at dawn with a winged heart and give thanks for another day of loving.

To rest at the noon hour and meditate love's ecstasy.

To return home at eventide with gratitude.

And then to sleep with a prayer for the beloved in your heart and a song of praise upon your lips.

水般向夜晚吟唱优美的曲调；

明白过多的温柔所带来的苦痛；

情愿且快乐地为自己对爱的理解所伤害。

在黎明带着轻快的心醒来并感谢又一个有爱的日子；

在中午休息并品味爱的喜悦；

在黄昏怀着感恩的心回家；

然后为内心所爱之人祈祷，吟唱赞美之歌，并带着祷告和歌声入眠。

单词解析 *Word Analysis*

beckon ['bɛkən] v.（用头或手的动作）示意，召唤

例 The big time beckons to him.
辉煌时刻在向他召唤。

steep [stip] *adj.* 陡峭的，险峻的；过分的，夸张的；极高的；急剧升降的

例 San Francisco is built on 40 hills and some are very steep.
旧金山建在40座小山丘上，其中一些非常陡峭。

enfold [ɪn'foʊld] v. 围住……，抱紧……

例 Aurora felt the opium haze enfold her.
奥萝拉感觉自己被笼罩在鸦片烟霾中。

yield [jɪːld] *n.* 生产量，投资收益 *v.* 生产；同意；给予；出产；投降，屈服

例 We will never yield to force.
我们决不会向暴力屈服。

sword [sɔːrd] *n.* 剑，刀；武力，战争；兵权，权力

例 I parried, and that's when my sword broke.
我挡了一下，把我的剑挡断了。

shatter ['ʃætə] *v.* 使破碎，使碎裂，砸碎；使……成为泡影；使……痛不欲生；使……散开 *n.* 碎片，碎块；落花（叶等）

例 One bullet shattered his skull.
一颗子弹打穿了他的头颅。

crucify ['kruːsə,faɪ] *v.* 把（某人）钉死在十字架上；折磨，虐待；抑制，克制；处以钉在十字架的死刑

例 She'll crucify me if she finds you still here.
如果她发现你还在这儿，她会狠狠地教训我。

pruning [pruːnɪŋ] *n.* 修枝，剪枝，修剪 *v.* 修剪（树木等）（prune的现在分词）；精简某事物，除去某事物多余的部分

例 A sapling needs pruning, a child discipline.
小树要砍，小孩要管。

ascend [ə'sɛnd] *v.* 登高；追溯；上升；攀登；登上

例 The path started to ascend more steeply at this point.
这条路从这里向上就更陡了。

descend [dɪ'sɛnd] *v.* 下降；屈尊；传下

例 She descended the stairs.
她走下楼梯。

cling to 坚持；紧抓；保留；挨着

例 Some people had to cling to trees as the flash flood bowled them over.
一些人不得不紧紧抱住树干，因为湍急的洪水会把他们冲倒。

seek [si:k] *v* 寻找，探寻；追求，谋求；往或朝……而去；查找，查寻

例 They have had to seek work as laborers.
他们只好找体力活儿干。

nakedness ['neɪkɪdnəs] *n.* 裸露

例 We can now begin to see the difference between nakedness and nudity in the European tradition.
我们现在可以了解到在欧洲传统中裸体和裸像之间的区别。

naught [nɔt] *n.* 零；泡影；乌有

例 He sets at naught every convention of society.
他轻视所有的社会习俗。

desire [dɪ'zaɪə] *v* 渴望；希望；要求；请求 *n.* 欲望；愿望；希望；请求

例 I had a strong desire to help and care for people.
我非常渴望能够帮助和照顾他人。

melody ['mɛlədi] *n.* 歌曲；旋律，曲调；美妙的音乐，和谐的调子；好听的声音

例 Her voice was full of melody.
她的声音非常悦耳。

语法知识点 *Grammar Points*

① **When love beckons to you, follow her, though her ways are hard and steep.**

这个句子中有一个结构 "beckon to sb."，表示 "向……示意，召唤"。后面接动词不定式 beckon (to) sb. (to do sth.)。

例 She beckoned (to) me (to follow).
她招手要我跟着她。

② **Even as she ascends to your height and caresses your tenderest branches that quiver in the sun, so shall she descend to your roots and shake them in their clinging to the earth.**

这个句子中有一个结构 "ascend to"，表示 "升至，追溯到"。

例 He eventually ascended to the position of chief executive.
他最终升到了首席执行官的位置。

经典名句 *Famous Classics*

1. Every man is a poet when he is in love.
每个恋爱中的人都是诗人。

2. First love is only a little foolishness and a lot of curiosity.
初恋就是一点点笨拙外加许许多多好奇。

3. Friendship is like earthenware: once broken, it can be mended;
love is like a mirror: once broken, that ends it.
友谊就像陶器，破了可以修补；爱情好比镜子，一旦打破就难重圆。

4. Friendship is love without his wings.
友谊是没有羽翼的爱。

5. The greater the power, the more dangerous the abuse.
权力越大，滥用职权的危险就越大。

读书笔记

10 Loving with an Open Hand
放爱一条生路

The other day as I talked with a friend I recalled a story that I heard this summer: "A **compassionate** person, seeing a butterfly struggling to free itself from its **cocoon**, and wanting to help, very gently loosened the filaments to form an opening. The butterfly was freed, emerged from the cocoon, and fluttered about but could not fly. What the compassionate person did not know was that only through the birth struggle can the wings grow strong enough for flight. Its shortened life was spent on the ground; it never knew freedom, never really lived."

I call it learning to love with an open hand. It is a learning which has come slowly to me and has been wrought in the fires of pain and in the waters of patience. I am learning that I must free the one I love, for if I clutch or cling, try to control, I lose what I try to hold.

If I try to change someone I love because I feel I know how that person should be, I rob him or her of a precious right, the right to take **responsibility** for one's own life and choices and way of

前几天和一位朋友闲聊时，我想起今年夏天听到的一个故事："有个人很富有同情心，看到一只蝴蝶拼命挣扎想冲破茧的束缚，就帮了个忙，轻轻地解开茧丝使其露出一个缺口。蝴蝶得到解放，从茧中出来振翅欲飞，然而却飞不起来。这位富有同情心的人所不知道的是，蝴蝶只有经过挣扎破茧而出，翅膀才能变得强壮，可以飞翔。这只蝴蝶短暂的生命只能在地上度过了，它从未尝过自由的滋味，没有真正活过。"

我把这叫作学会放爱一条生路。这对于我来说是一次缓慢的学习，在经历了痛苦的锻造和耐心的洗礼后，我学会了必须给所爱的人自由，如果我抓得太牢、紧握不放、设法控制，结果可能会失去他。

如果我试图改变所爱的人，仅仅是因为我觉得他/她应该这样，就等于是掠夺了他/她一项珍贵的权利，即他/她对自己生命的责任权和生活方式的选择权。无论何时我把自己

being. Whenever I impose my wish or want or try to exert power over another, I rob him or her of the full realization of growth and maturation. I limit and prevent by my act of possession, no matter how kind my intention.

I can limit and injure by the kindest acts of protection or concern. Over extended it can say to the other person more **eloquently** than words "You are unable to care for yourself; I must take care of you because you are mine. I am responsible for you."

As I learn and practice more and more, I can say to the one I love: "I love you, I value you, I respect you and I trust that you have the strength to become all that it is possible for you to become—if I don't get in your way. I love you so much that I can set you free to walk beside me in joy and in sadness. I will share your tears but I will not ask you not to cry. I will respond to your needs. I will care and comfort you, but I will not hold you up when you can walk alone. I will stand ready to be with you in your grief and loneliness but I will not take it away from you. I will strive to listen to your meanings as well as your words, but I shall not always agree. Sometimes I will be angry and when I am, I will try to tell you openly so that I need not hate our differences or feel

的意志和权力强加给别人，都会导致他/她无法完全成长和成熟。无论我的意图多么善良，我的控制行为还是限制和阻碍了他们。

即使保护或关心这种最善意的行为也会限制和伤害别人。"你无法照顾自己，我必须照顾你，因为你是我的，我要对你负责。"对别人说这么动人的话语远远超越了你的权力。

随着学习和锻炼的增多，现在我会这样告诉我爱的人："我爱你、珍惜你、尊重你，我相信你有足够的实力发展成为你想要成为的人——如果我不阻碍你的话。我是那么爱你，所以我给你自由，在我身旁和我共享欢乐与悲伤。我会和你一起流泪，但我不会要求你停止哭泣。我会满足你的需要，关心你、安慰你，但在你能够独立行走时我不会阻挡你。我会时刻准备好，在你悲伤和孤独时站到你身边，但我不会把你的悲伤和孤独带走。我会尽力理解你的话语及其中含义，但不会总是赞同。有时我会生气，当我生气时，我会尽量坦率地告诉你，这样我就不会对我们之间的分歧怀恨于心，产生疏远的感觉。我无法

estranged. I can not always be with you or hear what you say for there are times when I must listen to myself and care for myself, and when that happens I will be as honest with you as I can be."

I am learning to say this, whether it be in words or in my way of being with others and myself, to those I love and for whom I care. And this I call loving with an open hand.

I cannot always keep my hands off the cocoon, but I am getting better at it!

时刻与你在一起，或者听你诉说，因为有时我需要倾听自己，关心自己，当这些发生时，我会尽量告诉你。"

对于那些我所爱和所关心的人，我正在学习这样表达，无论是用语言，还是用我对待他人及自己的方式，我把这叫作放爱一条生路。

我不会总把双手从茧的身旁移开，但我正在逐渐进步做得更好！

单词解析 *Word Analysis*

compassionate [kəmˈpæʃənɪt] *adj.* 有同情心的；表示怜悯的 *v.* 同情；怜悯

例 She has a wise, compassionate face.
她的脸上显露出智慧和同情。

cocoon [kəˈkun] *n.* 茧，蚕茧 *v.* 把……紧紧包住

例 He stood there in a cocoon of golden light.
他站在那儿，一柱金光笼罩着他。

responsibility [rɪˌspɑːnsəˈbɪləti] *n.* 责任；职责；责任感，责任心

例 No one admitted responsibility for the attacks.
没有人对这些袭击负责。

eloquently [ˈeləkwəntlɪ] *adv.* 善辩地，富于表现力地

例 The poet eloquently expresses the sense of lost innocence.
诗人动人地表达了失去天真的感觉。

estrange [ɪˈstrendʒ] *v.* 使疏远（尤指家庭成员之间）

例 His constant need to travel served to estrange him from most family activities.
他经常需要远游而无法参加大多数家人的活动。

语法知识点 *Grammar Points*

① The other day as I talked with a friend I recalled a story that I heard this summer: "A compassionate person, seeing a butterfly struggling to free itself from its cocoon, and wanting to help, very gently loosened the filaments to form an opening."

这个句子中有一个结构 "struggle to do"，表示 "尽力做某事"。相当于 try to do 和 strive to do sth.。这句话里有一个定语从句，I recalled a story 为主句，that 后面引导定语从句，修饰先行词 the story。

 She struggled to get away from her attacker.
她挣扎着想摆脱那个侵犯她的人。

② If I try to change someone I love because I feel I know how that person should be, I rob him or her of a precious right, the right to take responsibility for one's own life and choices and way of being.

这个句子中有两个结构 "rob sb. of sth." 和 "take responsibility for"，分别表示 "剥夺某人的某物，窃取某人的某物" 和 "为……负责"。

 I was robbed (of my cash and cheque-book).
我（的现金和支票簿）被抢了。

The manufacturers take no responsibility for damage caused by misuse.
使用不当而造成的损坏，生产厂家不负任何责任。

③ You are unable to care for yourself; I must take care of you because you are mine.

这个句子中有两个结构 "be unable to" 和 "take care of"，分别表示 "没有能力做某事" 和 "照顾"。后者相当于 look after。

 I tried to contact him but was unable to.
我竭力想与他联系，但是没联系上。

I will take care of you from now on.
从现在开始我来照顾你。

④ As I learn and practice more and more, I can say to the one I love: "I love you, I value you, I respect you and I trust that you have the strength to become all that it is possible for you to become—if I don't get in your way."

这句话里有两个结构 "have the strength to do" 和 "in one's way"，分别表示"有能力做某事"和"挡道，碍事"。

例 Jenny didn't have the strength to end the relationship.
詹妮没有能力结束这段关系。

Don't get in my way.
别挡我的道。

⑤ **I cannot always keep my hands off the cocoon, but I am getting better at it!**

这个句子中有一个结构 "keep one's hands off sth."，表示"不干涉某事"。

例 Please keep your hands off me.
请别管我！

经典名句 *Famous Classics*

1. It's not because of stability that someone wants to marry, but because of lack of stability.
并不是因为安定了，所以想要结婚；而是因为缺少安定，所以才要结婚。

2. It is graceful grief and sweet sadness to think of you, but in my heart, there is a kind of soft warmth that can't be expressed with any choice of words.
想你，是一种美丽的忧伤和甜蜜的惆怅，心里面，却是一种用任何语言也无法表达的温馨。

3. In this world, only those men who really feel happy can give women happiness.
在这个世界，只有真正快乐的男人才能带给女人幸福。

4. If you love a girl, it's better to fight for her happiness than to abandon her for the sake of her happiness.
爱一个女孩，与其为了她的幸福而放弃她，不如留住她，为她的幸福而努力。

5. If you leave me, please don't comfort me because each sewing has to meet stinging pain.
离开我就别安慰我，要知道每一次缝补也会遭遇穿刺的痛。

11 Letting Go
放手

There was once a lonely girl who longed **desperately** for love. One day while she was walking in the woods she found two **starving** songbirds. She took them home and put them in a small cage. She **nurtured** them with love and the birds grew strong. Every morning they greeted her with a **marvelous** song. The girl felt great love for the birds. She wanted their singing to last forever.

One day the girl opened the door of the cage. The larger and stronger of the birds flew from the cage. The girl watched **anxiously** as he circled high above her. She was so frightened that he would **fly away** and she would never see him again. As he flew close, she **grasped** him wildly. She caught him in her fist. Her heart **gladdened** at her success in capturing him. Suddenly she felt the bird go limp. She opened her hand and stared in horror at the dead bird. Her **desperate** clutching love had killed him.

She noticed the other bird **teetering** on the edge of the cage. She could feel his great need for freedom and his need to soar into the clear, blue sky. She lifted him from the cage and tossed him

从前，有一个孤独的姑娘，她非常渴望爱。一天，她在树林中散步时发现了两只快要饿死的鸟儿，她将它们带回家，放进了一个小笼子里。她用爱滋养着它们，两只鸟渐渐强健起来。每天早晨，它们都要唱一首动听的歌曲问候她。姑娘很喜欢这两只鸟，她想让它们的歌一直唱下去。

有一天，姑娘打开鸟笼的门，其中那只比较强壮的大鸟从笼子里飞了出去。它在姑娘的头顶高高盘旋。姑娘不安地望着，她害怕它会飞走，再也看不到它，所以当它飞近时，她疯狂地去抓它。她紧紧地把它抓在手里。她的心因成功地捕到它而愉悦。突然，她伸开手，惊恐地发现鸟儿已经死去了。她不顾一切、牢牢紧握的爱扼杀了它。

她注意到另一只鸟在笼边不断徘徊。她能感觉到它对自由的极度渴望，对翱翔于蓝天白云下的渴望。她从笼子里把它取出来，将它轻轻地抛向空中。鸟儿绕了一圈，一圈，

soft into the air. The bird circled once, twice, three times. The girl watched delightedly at the bird flying cheerfully. Her heart was no longer concerned with her loss. She wanted the bird to be happy. Suddenly the bird flew closer and landed softly on her shoulder. It sang the sweetest melody she had ever heard.

The fastest way to lose love is to hold on too tight while the best way to keep love is to give it—WINGS!

又一圈。姑娘高兴地看着小鸟快乐地飞翔。她不再关心她的所失，她只想要小鸟快活。突然，小鸟飞近了，轻轻地落在她的肩上，唱起她有生以来听过的最甜美的旋律。

失去爱的最快途径是紧抓不放，而留住爱的最佳途径是给它——翅膀！

单词解析 *Word Analysis*

desperately ['dɛspərɪtlɪ] *adv.* 绝望地；不顾一切地；<口>极度地；猛烈地

例 He desperately needed money.
他迫切需要钱。

starving ['stɑrvɪŋ] *adj.* 挨饿的；饥饿，引申为供应不足 *v.* （使）挨饿，饥饿（starve的现在分词）；缺乏，急需

例 Apart from anything else I was starving.
别的不说，我饿坏了。

nurture ['nɜːrtʃə(r)] *v.* 培育；养育；滋养；培植 *n.* 教养，培育；营养物，食物；环境因素

例 Charlie Nelson has nurtured fine sprinters.
查理·纳尔逊已经培养出了相当优秀的短跑选手。

marvelous ['mɑrvələs] *adj.* 不可思议的；非凡的；引起惊异的；神乎其神的

例 It seems to me a most marvelous book.
我觉得这本书奥妙之至。

anxiously ['æŋkʃəslɪ] *adv.* 焦急地，担忧地；眼巴巴地

例 He frowned at her anxiously.
他不安地朝她皱了皱眉。

fly away 飞走

例 That bird flew away yesterday.
那只鸟昨天飞走了。

grasp [græsp] *v.* 抓住；了解；急切（或贪婪）地抓住 *n.* 控制；控制力；能力所及

例 They have a good grasp of foreign languages.
他们外语掌握得很好。

gladden ['glædn:] *v.* 使高兴，使快乐

例 Charles's visit surprised him and gladdened him.
查尔斯的来访让他惊喜交加。

desperate ['dɛspərɪt] *adj.* 绝望的；由绝望而引起的；铤而走险的，孤注一掷的；急切的，极度渴望的

例 He made a desperate attempt to hijack a plane.
他铤而走险，企图劫持一架飞机。

teeter ['titə] *v.* 摇晃，蹒跚；犹豫不决；使……上下晃动 *n.* 跷跷板；踉跄，摇摆

例 His voice teetered on the edge of hysteria.
他的声音近乎歇斯底里。

语法知识点 *Grammar Points*

① **There was once a lonely girl who longed desperately for love. One day while she was walking in the woods she found two starving songbirds.**

这个句子中有一个结构"long for sth."，表示"渴望，向往"。注意，long 后面接动词不定式to do sth.。

例 She longed to see him again.
她渴望再看到他。

② **She opened her hand and stared in horror at the dead bird.**

这个句子中有两个结构"stare at"和"in horror"，分别表示"盯着看"

和"惊恐地"。一般表示注视或者看的意思时，动词常与介词at连用，如look at、glance at 和 glare at。

例 Don't stare at people like that; it's rude.
别那样盯着人看，太粗鲁了。

The crowd cried out in horror as the car burst into flames.
车爆炸起火的瞬间，人群惊恐地大叫起来。

③ She noticed the other bird teetering on the edge of the cage.

这个句子中有一个结构"on the edge of"，表示"在……的边缘"。相当于on the verge of。

例 They built the church on the edge of the village.
他们在小镇边缘建起了教堂。

④ Her heart was no longer concerned with her loss.

这个句子中有两个结构"no longer"和"be concerned with"，分别表示"不再"和"与……相关；担心"。前者相当于not any longer；后者相当于be worried about。

例 The cinema is no longer used.
这个电影院不再开了。

All the people are concerned with children's education.
孩子的教育是所有人都关心的问题。

经典名句 Famous Classics

1. Love is hard to get into, but harder to get out of.
爱很难投入，但更难走出。

2. Love is a light that never dims.
爱是一盏永不会昏暗的明灯。

3. He who has never loved, has never lived.
人活着总要爱一回。

4. Life is the flower and love is the honey.
生命如花，爱情是蜜。

5. No words are necessary between two loving hearts.
两颗相爱的心之间不需要言语。

12 In Giving I Connect with Others
给予连接你和我

I have lived with passion and in a hurry, trying to accomplish too many things. I never had time to think about my beliefs until my 28-year-old daughter Paula fell ill. She was in a **coma** for a year and I took care of her at home, until she died in my arms in December of 1992.

During that year of **agony** and the following year of my grieving, everything stopped for me. There was nothing to do—just cry and remember. However, that year also gave an opportunity to reflect upon my journey and the principles that hold me together. I discovered that there is consistency in my beliefs, my writing and the way I lead my life. I have not changed. I am still the same girl I was fifty years ago, and the same young woman I was in the seventies. I still **lust** for life, I am still **ferociously** independent, I still crave justice and I fall madly in love easily.

Paralyzed and silent in her bed, my daughter Paula taught me a lesson that is now my **mantra**: You only have what you give. It's by spending yourself that you become rich.

生活中我总是充满激情，忙忙碌碌，有太多的事想做。直到我二十八岁的女儿保拉病倒，我才有时间思考我的信仰。她昏迷了整整一年，我在家照顾她，直到1992年12月，她在我怀中死去。

在那一年的痛苦和接下来整整一年的悲恸中，一切都停止了，我什么都做不了——只剩哭泣和回忆。然而，那一年也使我得以回顾走过的人生，思考那些支撑我的信念。我发现我的信念原则、我的作品风格和我的生活方式始终如一。我没有改变，仍是五十年前那个女孩，仍是七十年代的那个姑娘。我渴望真正的生活，极端的独立，追求正义，轻易陷入热恋之中。

瘫痪在床、昏迷不醒的女儿教会我并使我坚信：给予什么，你就会收获什么。只有付出才能使人富有。

女儿的一生都在付出。她是一个帮助妇女和儿童的志愿者，每天工作8小时，每周工作6天。收入微薄，但她所求

Paula led a life of service. She worked as a volunteer helping women and children, eight hours a day, six days a week. She never had any money, but she needed very little. When she died she had nothing and she needed nothing. During her illness I had to let go of everything: her laughter, her voice, her grace, her beauty, her company and finally her spirit. When she died I thought I had lost everything. But then I realized I still had the love I had given her. I didn't even know if she was able to receive that love. She could not respond in any way; her eyes were somber pools that reflected no light. But I was full of love and that love kept growing and multiplying and giving fruit.

The pain of losing my child was a cleansing experience. I have to throw overboard all excess baggage and keep only what is essential. Because of Paula, I don't cling to anything anymore. Now I like to give much more than to receive. I am happier when I love than when I am loved. I **adore** my husband, my son, my grandchildren, my mother, my dog, and frankly I don't know if they even like me. But who cares? Loving them is my joy.

Give, give, give—what is the point of having experience, knowledge or talent if I don't give it away? Of having

甚少。她在去世的时候一无所有，也一无所求。卧床期间，我眼睁睁地看着她的一切都离我远去：她的笑貌，她的音容，她的婉约，她的娇美，她的陪伴，甚至她的灵魂。当她去世的时候，我以为我已经一无所有了，可后来我意识到，我仍然拥有给她的爱。我甚至不知道那个时候她是否能感受到我的爱。她无法做出任何反应，她的双眼就像死沉的水潭，没有一丝光泽。但我心中充满了爱。这种爱生生不息，开花结果。

失去爱女之痛对我而言是一种净化。我必须剔除那些无谓的累赘，留下生命的精髓。因为女儿，我不再是那个什么事情都放不下的人。如今，我希望给予甚于受赠。爱人比被爱更让我欣喜。我爱丈夫、爱儿子、爱孙子、爱母亲、爱我的狗。说实话，我甚至都不知道他们到底喜不喜欢我。但我不在乎，爱他们足以使我开心。

给予、给予、给予——如果不给予，那些经验、学识和天赋有何意义？如果不讲述，那些经历过的故事有何意义？如果不分享，那些财富又有何意义？我并不打算将给予带进棺材。在给予中，我与他人紧

stories if I don't tell them to others? Of having wealth if I don't share it? I don't intend to be cremated with any of it! It is in giving that I connect with others, with the world and with the divine.

It is in giving that I feel the spirit of my daughter inside me, like a soft presence.

紧相连，与世界紧紧相连，与上帝紧紧相连。

在给予中，我仿佛感到身旁女儿的灵魂如同一个温柔的存在般仍然与我紧紧相连。

单词解析 *Word Analysis*

coma ['koʊmə] *n.* <医>昏迷；怠惰，麻木；<天>（彗星的）彗发

例 She was in a coma for seven weeks.
她已经昏迷7个星期了。

agony ['ægəni] *n.* 极大的痛苦；苦恼，烦闷；临死的挣扎；（感情的）迸发

例 A new machine may save thousands of animals from the agony of drug tests.
一种新型机器也许可以将成千上万的动物从药物试验的痛苦中解救出来。

lust [lʌst] *n.* 色欲；强烈的欲望；渴望，热烈追求 *v.* 好色；渴望；贪求

例 It was Fred's lust for glitz and glamour that was driving them apart.
是弗雷德对浮华、奢靡生活的强烈欲望使他们越走越远。

ferociously [fə'roʊʃəslɪ] *adv.* 野蛮地，残忍地

例 He trapped Conn in a corner and pummeled him ferociously for thirty seconds.
他将康恩逼进一个角落，用拳头暴打了他半分钟。

mantra ['mæntrə] *n.* 咒语；颂歌，圣歌

例 Listening to customers is now part of the mantra of new management in public services.
倾听顾客意见现在已成了公共事业机构每一届新管理层都会奉行的准则之一。

adore [ə'dɔr,ə'dor] 崇拜；爱慕；非常喜欢；敬佩

例 She adored her parents and would do anything to please them.
她很爱自己的父母，为让他们高兴愿意做任何事。

语法知识点 *Grammar Points*

① **I never had time to think about my beliefs until my 28-year-old daughter Paula fell ill.**

这句话中有一个结构 "have time to do sth."，表示 "有时间做某事"。该句中用了not...until...，表示 "直到……才……"。

例 I have a lot of time to be with you.
我有很多时间和你在一起。

② **However, that year also gave an opportunity to reflect upon my journey and the principles that hold me together.**

这句话中有三个结构 "however"、"an opportunity to do" 和 "reflect upon"，分别表示 "但是，无论如何"、"一个做某事的机会" 和 "反思"。其中，however的同义词还有yet、but、nevertheless、notwithstanding等；reflect upon相当于reflect on。

例 I thought those figures were correct. However, I have recently heard they were not.
我原以为那些数字正确无误，不过我最近听说并不正确。

Everyone will have an opportunity to comment.
每人都有机会评价。

I need time to reflect (on your offer/on what you offered).
我需要时间来考虑（你的建议/你提出的建议）。

③ **I still lust for life, I am still ferociously independent, I still crave justice and I fall madly in love easily.**

这个句子中有两个结构 "lust for" 和 "fall in love"，分别表示 "渴望" 和 "坠入爱河"。前者相当于crave for。

例 He lusted for revenge.
他渴望复仇。

I thought I was falling in love.

我觉得我坠入爱河了。

④ **She worked as a volunteer helping women and children, eight hours a day, six days a week.**

这个句子中有一个结构"work as"，表示"担任，以……身份工作"。同义词还有serve as。

例 I work as an English teacher.

我是一名英语教师。

⑤ **Because of Paula, I don't cling to anything anymore.**

这个句子中有两个结构"because of"和"cling to"，分别表示"由于"和"坚持，依附，紧握不放"。前者同义词还有due to；后者同义词是stick to。

例 I left because of them.

由于他们我离开了。

The mud clung to my shoes.

泥粘在我的鞋子上。

⑥ **It is in giving that I connect with others, with the world and with the divine.**

这个句子中有一个结构"connect with"，表示"连接"。该句包含一个强调句型It is...that...。

例 As people connect with each other, they are able to share their expertise and learn from others.

当人们彼此相连时，便能够共享专业技术，并互相学习。

经典名句 *Famous Classics*

1. Fear not that the life shall come to an end, but rather fear that it shall never have a beginning.
不要害怕生活会结束，应该担心的是生活从未真正开始。

2. Four short words sum up what has lifted most successful individuals above the crowd: a little bit more.

成功的秘诀就是四个简单的字：多一点点。

3. We improve ourselves by victories over ourselves. There must be contests, and we must win.
   我们通过战胜自己来改进自我。一定要有竞赛，我们一定要赢！

4. All things in their being are good for something.
   天生我材必有用。

5. Giving is a reward in itself.
   给予本身就是一个奖赏。

读书笔记

13 Damaged Goods
受损的物品

The dust **mites** danced in the **ray** of sunshine that provided the only light in the Rabbi's office. He leaned back in his office chair and sighed as he stroked his beard. Then he took his wire-rimmed glasses and polished them absent-**mindedly** on his flannel shirt.

"So," he said, "you were divorced. Now you want to marry this good Jewish boy. What's the problem?"

He **nestled** his **grizzled** chin in his hand and smiled softly at me.

I want to **shriek**. What's the problem? First of all, I'm Christian. Second, I'm older than he is. Third—and not least, by any means—I'm divorced! Instead, I looked back into his soft brown eyes and tried to form the words.

"Don't you think," I stuttered, "that being divorced is like being used? Like being damaged goods?"

He settled back into the office chair and stretched so that he was looking at the ceiling. He stroked the **scraggly** beard that covered his chin and his neck. Then, he returned to his spot behind the desk and leaned toward me.

"Say you have to have surgery. Say

微尘在射进拉比办公室的那缕阳光中飞舞着，那缕阳光是拉比办公室里唯一的光源。拉比坐在椅子上往后仰，抚摸着他的胡须叹息了一声。随后他摘下金丝眼镜，漫不经心地在法兰绒衬衫上擦拭着。

"这么说，"他开了口，"你离婚了。现在你想与这位犹太小伙结婚，有什么问题？"

他用手把住他那有花白胡须的下巴，温柔地冲我微笑着。

我真想尖叫。有什么问题？第一，我是基督教徒。第二，我比他年龄大。第三，也是最重要的一点——我离过婚！但我没有叫，而是迎向他那双温柔的棕色眼睛，努力组织着话语。

"您不认为，"我结结巴巴地说，"离过婚就像东西被用过一样吗？就像是受损的物品吗？"

他坐在椅子上，头往后靠，伸直了腿，将目光投向天花板。他轻抚着他那稀稀拉拉的、遮盖了下巴和脖子的胡须，然后他将身子转回办公桌

you have a choice between two doctors. Who are you going to choose? The one right out of medical school or the one with experience?"

"The one with experience." I said.

His face **crinkled** into a grin. "I would, too." he locked his eyes with mine. "So in this marriage, you will be the one with experience. That's not such a bad thing, you know."

"Often, marriages tend to drift. They get caught in dangerous currents. They get off course and head toward hidden **sandbars**. No one notices until it is too late. On your face, I see the pain of a marriage gone bad. You will notice the **drift** in this marriage. You'll call out when you see the rocks. You'll **yell** to watch out and pay attention. You'll be the person with experience." he sighed. "And believe me, that's not such a bad thing. Not bad at all."

He walked to the window and **peeked** between the **slats** of the blinds. "You see, no one here knows about my first wife. I don't hide it, but I don't make a big deal about it. She died early in our marriage before I moved here. Now, late at night I think of all the words I never said; I think of all the chances I let pass by in that first marriage, and I believe I'm a better husband to my wife today because of

前并朝我这边俯过来。

"比如说你得做个手术。有两位医生可供你选择。你会选谁？选刚从医学院毕业的，还是选有经验的？"

"有经验的那位。"我回答。

他笑了，脸上满是皱纹。"我也是，"他凝视着我说，"那么在这桩婚姻中，你就是有经验的一方。要知道这并不是什么坏事。"

"婚姻往往像在水上漂流，会陷入危险的激流里，会偏离航向流向暗藏的沙洲。等注意到时已经晚了。在你的脸上，我看到了一桩失败婚姻留下的痛苦。在这桩新婚姻中你会注意到流向。当你看到岩石时你会大喊一声，你会呼叫要小心些，注意点。你将是有经验的那个人。"他叹息着说，"相信我，那并不是什么坏事，真的不是。"

他走到窗边，透过百叶窗向外瞥了一眼。"你瞧，这里没有人知道我的第一个妻子。我并没有掩藏，但我也没有大肆渲染。我们结婚没多久她就去世了，后来我迁居到这里。现在，夜深人静时我想到所有那些我从未能说出的话，我想到所有那些我在第一次婚姻中错过的机会。我相信对于我现

the woman I lost."

For the first time, the sadness in his eyes had meaning. Now I understood why I chose to come to talk to this man about marriage instead of taking an easier route and getting married outside both our religions. The word "Rabbi" means teacher. Somehow I sensed he could teach me, or even lend me, the courage I needed in order to try again, to marry again and to love again.

"I will marry you and your David," said the Rabbi, "If you promise me that you will be the person who yells out when you see the marriage is in danger."

I promised him I would, and I rose to leave.

"By the way," he called to me as I hesitated in his doorway, "did anyone ever tell you that Joanna is a good Hebrew name?"

Sixteen years have passed since the Rabbi married David and me on a rainy October morning. And, yes, I have called out several times when I sensed we were in danger. I would tell the Rabbi how well his analogy has served me, but I cannot. He died two years after our wedding. But I will always be grateful for the priceless gift he gave me: the wisdom to know that all of our experiences in life make us not less valuable, but more valuable, not less

在的妻子而言，我能成为一个更好的丈夫，是因为那个我失去的女人。"

第一次，他眼里的悲伤显露出了含意。现在我明白了为什么我选择来和这个人谈论婚姻，而没有图省事去找不属于我们双方宗教的人为我们主持婚礼。"拉比"一词意味着老师。不知怎的，我感觉到他能教给我，甚至给予我再次尝试、再次结婚、再次奉献出爱情所需要的勇气。

"我会为你和你的戴维主持婚礼，"拉比说，"但条件是，你要答应我，当你发现婚姻陷入危机时你要大声说出来。"

我答应他我会的，然后起身离开。

"顺便说一句，"当我走到门口犹豫片刻时他叫住我，"有没有人告诉过你乔安娜是个很好的希伯来语名字？"

十月一个下雨的早晨，拉比为我和戴维主持了婚礼。一晃十六年过去了。是的，有几次当我感觉到我们身陷危机时我就大声地说了出来。我多想告诉拉比他的比喻让我多么受益。但是我无法告诉他。我们结婚两年后他就去世了。但是我永远感激他赐予我的无价的礼物：一种智慧。它让我懂得我们生活中

able to love, but more able to love.

所有的经历并不会让我们贬值，而是使我们更有价值，并不会让我们丧失爱的能力，而是让我们更有能力去爱。

单词解析 *Word Analysis*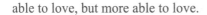

mite [maɪt] *n.* 小虫；极小量；小孩子；微小的东西

例 I can't help feeling just a mite uneasy about it.
我对此不禁感到一丝不安。

ray [reɪ] *n.* （热或其他能量的）射线；光束，光线 *v.* 放射；照射；（思想，希望等）闪现；发光

例 They could provide a ray of hope amid the general business and economic gloom.
在普遍的商业和经济低潮中，他们能带来一线希望。

minded ['maɪndɪd] *adj.* 有……思想的

例 The Home Office said at that time that it was minded to reject his application for political asylum.
那时候内政部称其准备驳回他的政治避难申请。

nestle ['nesəl] *v.* 安居，舒适地居住；偎依，贴靠；半隐半现地处于；[古语] 筑巢

例 Nearby, nestling in the hills, was the children's home.
孩子们的家就在附近的山里。

grizzle ['grɪzl] *n.* 灰色 *v.* 变成灰色；（尤指儿童）哭着不停地抱怨（某事）

例 All shades of red, wheaten, black and tan, or grizzle.
不同程度的红色、小麦色、黑色和棕色或灰色。

shriek [ʃriːk] *v.* 尖叫；引人注意 *n.* 尖叫声；尖锐的声音

例 "Stop it! Stop it!" shrieked Jane.
"停下！停下！"简尖叫道。

scraggly ['skrægli] *adj* 凸凹不平的；零乱的；锯齿状的；起伏的

例 He was very uptight about his daughter's scraggly-looking boyfriend.
他女儿那个外表邋遢的男朋友令他紧张不安。

crinkle ['krɪŋkəl] *v.* （使）起皱 *n.* （布或纸上的）皱纹

例 When she laughs, she crinkles her perfectly-formed nose.
她一笑，俊俏的鼻子就会皱起来。

drift [drɪft] *v.* 漂泊；流动；随意移动；浮现；漂流；聚积成堆

例 We proceeded to drift on up the river.
我们继续向河流的上游漂流。

sandbar ['sænd,bar] *n.* 沙洲

例 He jumped in the shallow limpid water of the white sandbar.
他跳进了白沙滩上那片清澈透底的水里。

peek [pik] *v.* 偷看，窥视；眯着眼睛看 *n.* 偷看，窥视；一瞥，看一眼

例 On two occasions she had peeked at him through a crack in the wall.
她曾两次透过墙缝窥视他。

slat [slæt] *n.* 板条，狭板 *v.* 用板条做或装备，打，猛投

例 Give me that piece of slat.
递给我那块板条。

yell [jɛl] *v.* 叫喊，大声叫；叫喊着说 *n.* 叫喊，大声叫；（啦啦队鼓动运动员的）呼喊声

例 Something brushed past Bob's face and he let out a yell.
有什么东西从鲍勃的脸上扫过，他大叫了一声。

语法知识点 *Grammar Points*

① First of all, I'm Christian.

这个句子中有一个结构"first of all"，表示"首先"。同义词还有firstly、at first 和 at the outset。

例 First of all we should chase these fears from his mind.
首先我们应当消除他心中的恐惧。

② Often, marriages tend to drift.

这个句子中有一个结构"tend to do"，表示"易于，有……的倾向"。同义词组还有have a tendency to do。

例 I tend to go to bed earlier during the winter.
我在冬天常睡得较早。

③ You'll yell to watch out and pay attention.

这个句子中有两个结构"watch out"和"pay attention"，分别表示"小心，提防"和"注意"。前者相当于be careful。

例 "Watch out!" he shouted.
他大叫道："小心！"

Please pay attention (to what I am saying).
请注意（我说的话）。

④ Now I understood why I chose to come to talk to this man about marriage instead of taking an easier route and getting married outside both our religions.

这个句子中有两个结构"choose to do"和"instead of doing"，分别表示"选择做某事"和"而不是做某事"。

例 We chose to go by train.
我们决定乘火车去。

Let's play cards instead of watching television.
咱们玩纸牌吧，别看电视了！

⑤ …If you promise me that you will be the person who yells out when you see the marriage is in danger.

这个句子中有一个结构"in danger"，表示"在危险中"。相当于in peril。

例 His life was in danger.
他有生命危险。

经典名句 *Famous Classics*

1. Love is the union of two souls.
爱情是两颗灵魂的结合。

2. Love is the salt of life.
爱情是生命的盐。

3. Love drag me to this side, but reason has to pull me to the other side.
爱情把我拽向这边，而理智却要把我拉向那边。

4. Love is easy to believe.
爱容易轻信。

5. Ordinary people merely think how they shall spend their time; a man of talent tries to use it.
普通人只想到如何度过时间，有才能的人设法利用时间。

读书笔记

14 Marriage, Love and Freedom
婚姻、爱与自由

You are asking, "Is it possible to be married and to be free?"

If you take marriage non-seriously, then you can be free. If you take it seriously, then freedom is **impossible**. Take marriage just as a game—it is a game. Have a little sense of humor, that it is a role you are playing on the stage of life; but it is not something that belongs to existence or has any reality—it is a **fiction**.

But people are so stupid that they even start taking fiction for reality. I have seen people reading fiction with tears in their eyes, because in the fiction things are going so tragically. It is a very good device in the movies that they put the lights off, so everybody can enjoy the movie, laughing, crying, being sad and being happy. If there is light it would be a little difficult-what will others think? And they know perfectly well that the screen is empty-there is nobody; it is just a **projected** picture. But they forget it completely.

And the same has happened with our lives. Many things which are simply to be taken humorously, we take so

你问："结婚后还保持自由，可能吗？"

轻松地看待婚姻，自由是可能的；严肃地看待婚姻，自由绝不可能。把婚姻就看作游戏——它是个游戏。多一点幽默感，它只是你在人生舞台上扮演的一个角色；并不存在，也没有真实性——它是虚构的。

但人们如此愚蠢，居然把虚构当作现实。我看见，人们读小说，悲惨的故事让他们流泪。播放电影时把灯关掉是一个很好的策略，这样每个人能享受这部电影，欢笑、哭泣、伤心或是快乐。要是灯开着，这就有点难——如果表露情绪，别人会怎么想？他们很清楚，屏幕里空无一物——没有人，只是投影的图像。但他们完全忘了这个事实。

我们的生活里，也会发生同样的事。很多事情，只需幽默看待，我们却那么严肃——结果问题纷至沓来。

首先，你为什么要结婚呢？你爱某人，与某人一起生活——这都是你的基本权利。

seriously-and from that **seriousness** begins our problem.

In the first place, why should you get married? You love someone, then live with someone—it is part of your basic rights. You can live with someone, you can love someone.

Marriage is not something that happens in heaven; it happens here, through the **crafty priests**. But if you want to join the game with society and don't want to stand alone and **aloof**, you make it clear to your wife or to your husband that this marriage is just a game: "Never take it seriously. I will remain as independent as I was before marriage, and you will remain as independent as you were before marriage. Neither I am going to **interfere** in your life, nor are you going to interfere in my life; we will live as two friends together, sharing our joys, sharing our freedom— but not becoming a **burden** on each other. And any moment we feel that the spring has passed, the **honeymoon** is over, we will be sincere enough not to go on pretending, but to say to each other that we loved much—and we will remain **grateful** to each other forever, and the days of love will **haunt** us in our memories, in our dreams, as golden— but the spring is over. Our paths have come to a point, where although it is

你能与某人一起生活，你能爱某人。

天堂里没有婚姻，婚姻只在尘世，通过牧师的狡诈而存在。但是，如果你不想超然独立，而想参与这个社会游戏，那么你就要让你的妻子或丈夫弄清楚，婚姻仅仅是个游戏："别把婚姻看得那么严肃。婚姻中，我将保持独立性，与婚前一样，你也是如此。你不妨碍我的生活，我也不妨碍你的生活；我们生活在一起，像两个好朋友，分享喜悦，分享自由——但绝不成为对方的负担。任何时刻，感觉到春天消失和蜜月结束，我们将足够真诚，绝不伪装，告诉对方：我们曾非常相爱——我们将对此永远保持感激，那些充满爱的时光，萦绕在我们的记忆和梦里，如黄金般宝贵——但现在春天结束了。我们已走到那个点，尽管令人伤心，但我们必须分开，因为现在，共同生活不再是爱的象征。如果我真的爱你，当看见我的爱让你痛苦时，我将离开你；如果你真的爱我，当你看见你的爱禁锢我时，你将离开我。"

爱是生命的最高价值：它不该蜕化为愚蠢的仪式。爱和自由如影随形——不可取舍。

sad, we have to part, because now, living together is not a sign of love. If I love you, I will leave you the moment I see my love has become a misery to you. If you love me, you will leave me the moment you see that your love is creating an **imprisonment** for me."

Love is the highest value in life: It should not be reduced to stupid **rituals**. And love and freedom go together—you cannot choose one and leave the other. A man who knows freedom is full of love, and a man who knows love is always willing to give freedom. If you cannot give freedom to the person you love, to whom can you give freedom? Giving freedom is nothing but trusting. Freedom is an expression of love.

So whether you are married or not, remember, all marriages are fake—just social **conveniences**. Their purpose is not to imprison you and bind you to each other; their purpose is to help you to grow with each other. But growth needs freedom; and in the past, all the cultures have forgotten that without freedom, love dies.

You see a bird on the **wing** in the sun, in the sky, and it looks so beautiful. Attracted by its beauty, you can catch the bird and put it in a golden cage.

Do you think it is the same bird? **Superficially**, yes, it is the same bird

知道自由的人充满了爱，知道爱的人总会给予自由。如果你不能给你所爱的人自由，那你又能把自由给谁呢？给予自由不是别的，就是信任。自由是爱的表达。

所以无论你是否结婚，记住，一切婚姻都是捏造品——仅仅为了社会的方便。婚姻的意图，不是让你们彼此囚禁和束缚，而是让你们彼此帮助，共同成长。但成长需要自由；在过去，所有文化都遗忘了一点：没有自由，爱将消失。

你看见一只鸟在阳光灿烂的天空中飞翔，多么美！它的美吸引着你，你可以捉住它，把它放进金鸟笼里。

你认为它还是原来那只鸟吗？表面上，它还是那只在天空中飞翔的鸟，但是，实际上它已经不是原来那只鸟——因为，没有它的天空，哪来它的自由？

这个金鸟笼对你而言，也许有价值；对鸟而言，毫无价值。在鸟看来，空中的自由飞翔，才是它生命中唯一的价值。对于人类，也是同样的道理。

who was flying in the sky; but deep down it is not the same bird—because where is its sky, where is its freedom?

This golden cage may be valuable to you; it is not valuable to the bird. For the bird, to be free in the sky is the only valuable thing in life. And the same is true about human beings.

单词解析 Word Analysis

impossible [ɪm'pɑːsəbl] *adj.* 不可能的，做不到的；难以忍受的 *n.* 不可能；不可能的事

例 The Government was now in an almost impossible position.
政府现在几乎陷入了进退维谷的境地。

fiction ['fɪkʃən] *n.* 小说，虚构的文学作品；编造，虚构

例 The truth or fiction of this story has never been truly determined.
这个故事一直以来真伪难辨。

project ['prɑːdʒekt] *v.* 计划；放映；发射；展现，使突出；伸出，突出 *n.* 项目，工程；计划，规划；（学生的）课题

例 Students complete projects for a personal tutor, working at home at their own pace.
学生完成了做私人家教的课题，在家里按自己的步调工作。

seriousness ['sɪriəsnəs] *n.* 认真；严肃性；严重性

例 He underrated the seriousness of William's head injury.
他低估了威廉头部伤势的严重性。

crafty ['kræfti] *adj.* 狡猾的，狡诈的；巧妙的，灵巧的 *adv.* 狡猾地，狡诈地 *n.* 狡猾，狡诈

例 That was my crafty little plan.
那是我的小妙计。

priest [prist] *n.* 神甫；神父，牧师 *v.* 使成为神职人员

例 He had been trained to be a Catholic priest.
他受训成为了一名天主教神父。

aloof [ə'luf] *adj.* 冷淡的；疏远的；远离的 *adv.* 分开地；避开地

例 I will hold myself aloof from wrong and corruption.
我会让自己远离错误和腐败。

interfere [,ɪntər'fɪr] *v.* 干预，干涉；调停，排解；妨碍，打扰

例 Drug problems frequently interfered with his work.
吸毒问题频频干扰他的工作。

burden ['bɜ:rdn] *n.* 负担，包袱；责任，义务；载货量 *v.* 使烦恼，劳累；向（车，船等）上装货

例 We decided not to burden him with the news.
我们决定不拿这个消息去烦他。

honeymoon ['hʌni,mun] *n.* 蜜月；蜜月期；蜜月旅行；短暂的和谐时期 *v.* 度蜜月

例 They honeymooned in Venice.
他们在威尼斯度了蜜月。

grateful ['gretfəl] *adj.* 感激的，感谢的；令人愉快的；宜人的

例 I'm ever so grateful.
我太感激了。

haunt [hɔnt,hant] *v.* 时常萦绕心头，使困窘；常去；以鬼魂形式出现；时常出现在，弥漫 *n.* 〈方〉鬼或其他超自然物体；常去的地方

例 The stigma of being a bankrupt is likely to haunt him for the rest of his life.
破产的耻辱可能会让他余生不得安宁。

imprisonment [ɪm'prɪznmənt] *n.* 关押，监禁

例 She was sentenced to seven years' imprisonment.
她被判处7年监禁。

ritual ['rɪtʃuəl] *n.* 典礼；（宗教等的）仪式；例行公事，老规矩 *adj.* 作为仪式一部分的；礼节性的；例行公事的

例 The whole Italian culture revolves around the ritual of eating.
整个意大利的文化都以饮食为中心。

convenience [kən'viniəns] *n.* 方便，便利；便利设施；个人的舒适或利益；（公共）厕所

例 Like working women anywhere, Asian women are buying convenience foods.
像其他地方的职业女性一样，亚洲女性也购买方便食品。

wing [wɪŋ] *n.* 翅膀，翼；飞翔；派系，派别 *v.* 飞行；为……装上翼；使或使能飞行；飞过

例 We were given an office in the empty west wing.
我们在空置的大楼西翼分得了一间办公室。

superficially ['supə'fɪʃəlɪ] *adv.* 浅薄地，表面上地

例 It is superficially a concept problem, but actually a problem of profit.
表面上是一个观念问题，实质上是一个利益问题。

语法知识点 *Grammar Points*

① **Have a little sense of humor, that it is a role you are playing on the stage of life; but it is not something that belongs to existence or has any reality—it is a fiction.**

这个句子中有两个结构 "play a role" 和 "belong to"，分别表示 "扮演……角色" 和 "属于"。

例 He was invited to play a role in this TV play.
他受邀在这个电视剧里扮演一个角色。

They want to belong to Europe.
他们想归属欧洲。

② **In the first place, why should you get married?**

这个句子中有一个结构 "in the first place"，表示 "首先，第一位是"。

相当于firstly、first of all 和 at first。

例 In the first place, you must rev it up to warm the engine.
　　首先你必须让发动机转起来预热。

③ **I will remain as independent as I was before marriage, and you will remain as independent as you were before marriage.**

这个句子中有一个结构"as...as...",表示"和……一样"。

例 He doesn't play half as well as his sister.
　　他演奏的水平不及他姐姐的一半。

④ **Their purpose is not to imprison you and bind you to each other; their purpose is to help you to grow with each other.**

这个句子中有一个结构"help sb. to do sth.",表示"帮助某人干某事"。注意,help sb. 后面也可以直接加do sth.。另外,该句中"bind sb. to"是一个固定搭配,表示"把……捆绑在……上,安排……,迫使(某人)遵守/服从(规章、命令等)"。在该句中表示捆绑在一起。

例 Please help me do housework.
　　请帮我做家务。

⑤ **It should not be reduced to stupid rituals.**

这个句子中有一个结构"be reduced to",表示"减少到,还原为"。

例 Government should be reduced to only one function: the protection of individual rights.
　　政府仅应保留一项职能：保护公民的个人权利。

经典名句 *Famous Classics*

1. The success of a marriage depends on two people, and a person can make it fail.
　　婚姻的成功取决于两个人，而一个人就可以使它失败。

2. Love can conquer all.
　　爱能征服一切。

3. Love is in a hurry, and so is it.
　　爱来得快，散得也快。

4. Love is the alias of understanding.
爱是理解的别名。

5. Love is a sweet pain.
爱是一种甜蜜的痛苦。

读书笔记

----

15 The Classical Dialogue of *Jane Eyre*
《简·爱》经典对白

Chapter 20

Rochester: Well, then Jane, call to aid your **fancy**—**suppose** you were no longer a girl well reared and disciplined, but a wild boy **indulged** from childhood upwards; imagine yourself in a remote foreign land; **conceive** that you there commit a capital error, no matter of what nature or from what motives, but one whose **consequences** must follow you through life and **taint** all your existence. Mind I don't say a CRIME; I am not speaking of shedding of blood or any other guilty act, which might make the perpetrator amenable to the law: my word is ERROR. The results of what you have done become in time to you utterly **insupportable**; you take measures to obtain relief: unusual measures, but neither unlawful nor **culpable**. Still you are **miserable**; for the hope has quitted you on the very confines of life: your sun at noon darkens in an eclipse, which you feel will not leave it till the time of setting. Bitter and base associations have become the sole food of your memory: you wander here and there, seeking rest in **exile**; happiness in

第20章

罗切斯特："那么好吧，简，发挥你的想象力吧——设想你不再是受过精心培养和教导的姑娘，而是从幼年时代起就放纵任性的男孩。想象你身处遥远的异国，假设你在那里铸成了大错，不管其性质如何、出于什么动机，它的后果殃及你一生，玷污你的生活。注意，我没有说'犯罪'，没有说流血或是其他犯罪行为，那样的话肇事者会被绳之以法，我用的字眼是'错误'。你行为的恶果，到头来使你绝对无法忍受。你采取措施以求获得解脱，这是非正常的措施，但既不是非法，也并非有罪。而你仍然感到不幸，因为希望在生活的边缘离你而去：你的太阳遇上日食，在正午就开始暗淡，你觉得不到日落不会有所改变。痛苦和卑贱的联想，成了你记忆的唯一粮食；你到处游荡，在放逐中寻求安逸，在享乐中寻觅幸福——我的意思是沉湎于无情的肉欲——它销蚀才智，摧残情

pleasure—I mean in heartless, sensual pleasure—such as dulls intellect and blights feeling. Heart-weary and soul-withered, you come home after years of voluntary banishment: you make a new acquaintance—how or where no matter; you find in this stranger much of the good and bright qualities which you have sought for twenty years, and never before encountered; and they are all fresh, healthy, without soil and without taint. Such society revives, regenerates; you feel better days come back—higher wishes, purer feelings; you desire to recommence your life, and to spend what remains to you of days in a way more worthy of an immortal being. To attain this end, are you justified in overleaping an obstacle of custom—a mere conventional impediment which neither your conscience sanctifies nor your judgement approves?

Chapter 23

Jane: Do you think I can stay to become nothing to you? Do you think I am an **automaton**?—a machine without feelings? And can bear to have my morsel of bread snatched from my lips, and my drop of living water dashed from my cup? Do you think, because I am poor, obscure, plain, and little, I am soulless and heartless? You think wrong!—I have as much soul as you—

感。在几年的自愿放逐以后，你心力交瘁地回到了家里，结识了一位新知——何时结识，如何结识，都无关紧要。在这位陌生人身上，你看到了很多出类拔萃的品质，为它们你已经寻寻觅觅二十来年，却终不可得。这些品质新鲜健康，没有污渍，没有斑点，这种交往使人复活，催人新生。你觉得好日子又回来了——志更高，情更真。你渴望重新开始生活，以一种更配得上不朽的灵魂的方式度过余生。为了达到这个目的，你是不是有理由越过习俗的藩篱——那种既没有得到你良心的认可、也不为你的见识所赞同的、纯粹因袭的障碍？"

第23章

简："你难道认为，我会留下来甘愿做一个对你来说无足轻重的人？你以为我是一架机器？——一架没有感情的机器？能够容忍别人把一口面包从我嘴里抢走，把一滴生命之水从我杯子里泼掉？难道就因为我一贫如洗、默默无闻、长相平庸、个子瘦小就没有灵魂，没有心肠了？你想错了！——我的心灵跟你一样丰富——我的心胸跟你一样充实！要是上帝赐予我一点姿色

and full as much heart! And if God had gifted me with some beauty and much wealth, I should have made it as hard for you to leave me, as it is now for me to leave you. I am not talking to you now through the medium of custom, **conventionalities**, nor even of mortal flesh; it is my spirit that addresses your spirit; just as if both had passed through the grave, and we stood at God's feet, are equal—as we are!

和充足的财富，我会使你同我现在一样难分难舍，我不是通过习俗、常规，甚至也不是血肉之躯同你说话，而是我的灵魂同你的灵魂在对话，就仿佛我们两人穿过坟墓，站在上帝脚下，彼此平等——本来就如此！"

单词解析 *Word Analysis*

fancy ['fænsi] *v.* 想象；设想；想要；猜想 *n.* 设想；想象力；爱好；怪想 *adj.* （构思者）奇特的；昂贵的；[美国俚语]真棒

例 What do you fancy doing, anyway?
你到底想干什么？

suppose [sə'pəuz] *v.* 认为；假定；猜想，推测；让（用于祈祷语气）

例 Suppose someone gave you an egg and asked you to describe exactly what was inside.
假设有人给了你一枚鸡蛋并要你准确描述鸡蛋里面有什么。

indulge [ɪn'dʌldʒ] *v.* 迁就，纵容；使满足；使（自己）沉溺于；使快乐

例 Only rarely will she indulge in a glass of wine.
她只是偶尔才喝杯红酒，让自己享受一下。

conceive [kən'siv] *v.* 怀孕；构思；想象，设想；持有

例 I just can't even conceive of that quantity of money.
那么多钱，我根本都无法想象。

consequence ['kɑːnsəkwens] *n.* 推论；结果，成果；[逻]结论；重要性

例 Her lawyer said she understood the consequences of her actions and was prepared to go to jail.

她的律师说她明白自己行为的后果，已有了入狱的心理准备。

taint [tent] *n.* 污点，污名；传染，腐败 *v.* 玷污；败坏；使变质；使污染

例 Opposition leaders said that the elections had been tainted by corruption.

反对派领导人说，选举已被贪污腐败所破坏。

insupportable [ˌɪnsə'pɔːrtəbl] *adj.* 忍耐不住的，不能忍受的

例 Too much spending on rearmament would place an insupportable burden on the nation's productive capacity.

过于庞大的重整军备开支会给国家的生产力带来难以承受的负担。

culpable ['kʌlpəbəl] *adj.* 应受谴责的，应受处罚的，有罪的

例 They held him culpable for the offence.

他们认为他有罪应受惩罚。

miserable ['mɪzərəbəl,'mɪzrə-] *adj.* 悲惨的；令人痛苦的；太少的；卑鄙的

例 I took a series of badly paid secretarial jobs which made me really miserable.

我做了几份薪酬微薄的秘书工作，这让我非常郁闷。

exile ['ɛg,zaɪl,'ɛk,saɪl] *v.* 放逐，流放；使背井离乡 *n.* 流放，放逐，流亡；长期离家（出国）；被流放者，背井离乡者

例 He is now living in exile in Egypt.

他目前流亡埃及。

automaton [ɔː'tɑːmətən] *n.* 自动机，机器人

例 I get sick of being thought as a political automaton.

我讨厌被看作政治机器。

conventionality [kənˌvenʃə'nælətɪ] *n.* 习俗；照惯例；因循性；恪守常规

例 Conventionality is not morality. Self-righteousness is not religion.

习俗不等于道德，自以为是也不是宗教。

语法知识点 *Grammar Points*

① **I am not speaking of shedding of blood or any other guilty act, which might make the perpetrator amenable to the law: my word is ERROR.**

这个句子中有两个结构"speak of"和"amenable to"，分别表示"谈到，论及"和"服从，受……检验"。

例 To speak of his death so regardlessly wounded her feelings.
这样不经意地谈到他的死，伤了她的感情。

② **You take measures to obtain relief.**

这个句子中有一个结构"take measures to do"，表示"采取措施或者行动做某事"。相当于 take actions to do。

例 Will China take measures to protect its investments in Egypt?
中方是否采取措施保护在埃及的投资项目？

③ **…you desire to recommence your life, and to spend what remains to you of days in a way more worthy of an immortal being.**

这个句子中有一个结构"desire to do"，表示"想要做某事"。相当于 have a desire to do sth. 和 want to do sth.。

例 I have long desired to meet them.
我一直渴望见到他们。

④ **And if God had gifted me with some beauty and much wealth, I should have made it as hard for you to leave me, as it is now for me to leave you.**

这个句子中有一个结构"be gifted with"，表示"有……的天赋"。

例 He was witty, amusing and gifted with a sharp business brain.
他聪明、幽默且极具商业头脑。

经典名句 *Famous Classics*

1. Do you think, because I am poor, obscure, plain, and little, I am soulless and heartless? You think wrong!—I have as much soul as you—and full as much heart!

难道就因为我一贫如洗、默默无闻、长相平庸、个子瘦小就没有灵魂，没有心肠了——你想错了！我的心灵跟你一样丰富，我的心胸跟你一样充实！

2. You know some birds are not meant to be caged, their feathers are just too bright.
   你知道，有些鸟儿是注定不会被关在樊笼里的，它们的每一片羽毛都闪耀着自由的光辉。

3. There is something inside, that they can't get to, that they can't touch. That's yours.
   那是一种内在的东西，他们抵达不了，也无法触及，那是你的。

4. Life is like a box of chocolates; you never know what you're gonna get.
   生命就像一盒巧克力，结果每每出人意料。

5. Miracles happen every day.
   奇迹每天都在发生。

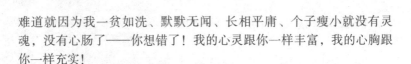

读书笔记

16 Roses from Heaven
来自天堂的玫瑰

Red roses were her favorites; her name was also Rose. And every year her husband sent her roses, tied with pretty bows. The year he died, the roses were still delivered to her door. The card said, "Be my **valentine**." like all the years before.

Each year he sent her roses, and the note would always say, "I love you even more this year, than last year on this day. My love for you will always grow, with every passing year." She knew this was the last time that the roses would appear.

She thought he ordered roses **in advance** before this day. Her loving husband did not know that he would pass away. He always liked to do things early, way before the time. Then, if he got too busy, everything would work out fine.

She **trimmed** the **stems**, placed them in a very special **vase**, then, set the vase beside the **portrait** of his smiling face. She would sit for hours, in her husband's favorite chair staring at his picture, with the roses sitting there.

A year went by, and it was hard to live without her **mate**. Loneliness and

红玫瑰是她的最爱，她的名字也叫玫瑰，每年他都会送给她玫瑰花，上面系着漂亮的蝴蝶结。他过世那年，玫瑰花仍然送到她家门口，玫瑰上的卡片像往年一样，照旧写着："送给我的恋人！"

以往每一年他送她玫瑰的时候，卡片总是写着："我爱你，今年的这一天要比去年的多，年复一年我对你的爱无时无刻不在心中滋长！"她知道这会是她最后一次收到玫瑰。

她想，他总是在情人节前几天预订玫瑰，她那充满爱心的丈夫不知道自己将会离开。他总喜欢提前安排好事情，这样，如果他忙起来的话，每一件事情也照样会进行得顺利。

她修剪了一下花的根部，把它们插进一个非常别致的花瓶里面，然后把花瓶安置在她丈夫遗照旁边，照片上的他面带微笑。她经常会坐在他最喜欢的椅子上，凝视着他那张照片，旁边就是那些玫瑰花。

就这样，一年过去了。没有爱人的日子是艰难的，只有

solitude had become her fate. Then, the very hour, as on Valentine's Day before, the doorbell rang, and there were roses, sitting by her door.

She brought the roses in, and just looked at them in shock. Then, she went to get the telephone and call the florist shop. The owner answered. She asked if he would explain why would someone do this to her, causing her such pain?

"I know your husband passed away, more than a year ago." The own said, "I know you'd call, and you would want to know. The flowers you received today were paid for in advance. Your husband always planned ahead; he left nothing to chance. There is a standing order, that I have one file down here, and he has paid, well in advance, you'll get them every year. There is also another thing that I think you should know: he wrote a special little card one year ago. Then, should ever, I find out that he's no longer here. That's the card that should be sent to you the following year." She thanked him and hung up the phone, her tears now flowing hard.

Her fingers shaking, as she slowly reached to get the card. Inside the card, she saw that he had written her a note. Then, as she stared in total silence, this is what he wrote:

"Hello my love, I know it's been

孤单和寂寞陪伴着她。情人节又一次到来的那个时刻，门铃响了，一束玫瑰花静静地躺在她的门口。

她把那束玫瑰花拿到屋里，惊讶地看着它们。然后走到电话前，拿起电话，拨通了花店的号码。店主接的电话。她问是否可以解释一下为什么会有人这样对她，让她如此痛苦。

花店老板说："我知道你丈夫一年前已经去世，我知道你会打电话问我是怎么回事。你今天收到的花是预订好的，你丈夫总是提前计划好一切，他从不会有任何侥幸心理。我这儿有个长期订单，就在这儿，你丈夫很早前就已付清，你会每年这个时候收到玫瑰花的。还有一件事你需要知道，他在一年多前写下了一张特殊的小卡片。接着，我就得知他过世的消息。这就是本应该在今年送给你的卡片。"她谢过店主，挂掉电话，眼泪不由自主地流了出来。

她手指颤动着缓慢地拿起那张卡片，在卡片里她看到了他留下的笔迹，她用静静的目光凝视着，上面写着：

"我的爱人，我知道我离开你有一年了。我希望，没有我的日子你依然过得很好。我知

a year since I've been gone. I hope it hasn't been too hard for you to overcome. I know it must be lonely, and the pain is very real. For if it was the other way, I know how I would feel. The love we shared made everything so beautiful in life. I loved you more than words can say; you were the perfect wife. You were my friend and lover; you fulfilled my every need. I know it's only been a year, but please try not to grieve. I want you to be happy, even when you shed your tears. That is why the roses will be sent to you for years. When you get these roses, think of all the happiness that we had together, and how both of us were blessed. I have always loved you and I know I always will. But, my love, you must go on; you have some living still. Please try to find happiness, while living out your days. I know it is not easy, but I hope you find some ways. The roses will come every year, and they will only stop, when your door's not answered, when the florist stops to knock. He will come five times that day, in case you have gone out. But after his last visit, he will know without a doubt, to take the roses to the place, where I've instructed him, and place the roses where we are, together once again."

道你现在很孤单，心很痛。如果我遭遇了这种事，如今也一定万分孤单和痛楚。我们共享的爱让生活中的一切变得如此美好。我无法用言语表达我有多么爱你，你是一个完美的妻子。你是我的朋友和爱人，你给予我所需要的一切。我知道仅仅过去了一年，但是请试着不要悲伤，我想要你快乐，甚至在你流下眼泪的时候。这就是我为什么要在以后每年送你玫瑰的原因。当你收到玫瑰的时候，想想我们在一起的快乐时光，我们都是如此幸运。我总是这样地爱你，将来也会如此！但是我的爱人，你必须走下去，你仍然需要生活。当我不在你身边的时候请试着寻找快乐，我知道这不容易，但是我希望你能用一些方法做到。玫瑰花每年都会送到，直到按你门铃没有人应答或花店关门，每年情人节他们会来五次，以免你不在。但是在第五次之后，他们就会确定，并把玫瑰拿到我指定的地方，在那里，我们会又一次相遇，并安详地躺在一起！"

单词解析 *Word Analysis*

valentine ['væhən,taɪn] *n.* 情人，心爱的人

例 Will you be my valentine?
你愿意做我的情人吗？

in advance [ɪnæd'væns] 提前；先期；在前头；预先，事先

例 Everything has been fixed in advance.
一切都是事先确定好了的。

trim [trɪm] *v.* 装饰；修剪；整理；削减 *adj.* 整齐的，整洁的；修长的；苗条的 *n.* 修剪；整齐；健康状态；装束

例 The neighbours' gardens were trim and neat.
邻居们的花园整洁美观。

stem [stɛm] *n.* （花草的）茎；（高脚酒杯的）脚；柄 *v.* 阻止；遏制（液体的流动等）；封堵；遏止

例 All my problems stem from drink.
我所有的问题都源于酗酒。

vase [veɪs] *n.* 装饰瓶，花瓶

例 You will catch it for breaking that vase.
你打破了那花瓶要挨骂了。

portrait ['pɔːtrət] *n.* 肖像，肖像画；模型，标本；半身雕塑像；人物描写

例 Lucian Freud has been asked to paint a portrait of the Queen.
卢西恩·弗洛伊德已受邀为女王画肖像画。

mate [meɪt] *n.* （工人间的）伙伴，同事，老兄，老弟；配偶，动物之偶（尤指鸟类） *v.* （使）成为配偶；（使）交配；（一对动物或鸟）交配；交尾(~ with sth)

例 He's off drinking with his mates.
他跟哥儿们出去喝酒了。

语法知识点 *Grammar Points*

① The year he died, the roses were still delivered to her door.

这句话里有一个结构"deliver...to...",表示"把……送到……"。

例 A courier delivered the parcels (to our office).
送急件的人将包裹送来（送到我们办公室）了。

② She thought he ordered roses in advance before this day.

这句话中有一个结构"in advance",表示"提前,预先"。相当于before hand 和 ahead of time。

例 If there is any change about the time of the meeting, please notify us in advance.
开会时间如有变,请提前告诉我们。

③ A year went by, and it was hard to live without her mate.

这句话中有一个结构"it's hard to do sth.",表示"干某事有困难"。相当于"it's difficult to do sth."。

例 So, it's hard for me not to see this as being political.
所以对我来说,很难不把这件事看作是一个政治事件。

④ I know your husband passed away, more than a year ago.

这句话中有一个结构"more than",表示"超过,多于",相当于over。

例 That would be more than I have expected.
那已经比我期望的还要多了。

⑤ He will come five times that day, in case you have gone out.

这句话中有一个结构"in case",表示"万一,假使"。

例 Do tell us in case you have any trouble.
万一有什么困难,一定告诉我们。

经典名句 *Famous Classics*

1. When alive, we may probably offend some people. However, we must think about whether they are deserved offended.
   人活着总是要得罪一些人的,但是要看那些人是否值得得罪。

2. You will have it if it belongs to you, whereas you don't ask for it if it doesn't appear in your life.

命里有时终需有，命里无时莫强求。

3. Eternity is not a distance but a decision.

永远不是一种距离，而是一种决定。

4. Dreaming in the memory is not as good as waiting for the paradise in the hell.

在回忆里继续梦幻，不如在地狱里等待天堂。

5. The darkness is no darkness with you.

有了你，黑暗不再是黑暗。

读书笔记

17 Blue Love
蓝色恋情

I just **separated** with Blue. Blue is a very nice girl, beautiful and gentle. Many friends said that I was a fool to let her go. Even though it was hard, I still had to let her go.

The 1st day

Using her blanket and covering herself tightly, she didn't get up. Her dorm mates were afraid to go in and comfort her. She didn't eat anything the whole day, didn't wash her face or brush her teeth. At night, I could hear her crying **beneath** the blanket.

The 2nd day

She ate today, forced down by her roommates. Her eyes were red. I always called her "cry baby". She always **squirmed** her mouth and retorted: "No, I'm not."

The 3rd day

Today, she dressed very sexy, walked into a bar and drank a lot of alcohol. Using tempting moves, she surveyed the room. Many men came up to her and **flirted** with her telling her how beautiful she was. She drank a lot more. When a much older man, old enough to be her father, walked up and said: "Miss, let me take you home."

刚和蓝分手。蓝是个很好的女孩，漂亮且温柔。很多朋友说我很傻，傻得离开她。虽然舍不得，可我还是放手了。

第一天

她没有起床，用被子把自己捂得严严实实的，宿舍的人都不敢去安慰她。她一天没有吃饭，连脸都没洗，牙也没刷，晚上睡觉的时候我听到她在被子里抽泣。

第二天

今天她吃饭了，是她的舍友逼着她吃的。她的眼眶红红的。我总说她是个爱哭鬼，她每次都撅着小嘴说她不是。

第三天

今天她穿得很妖艳，走进一家酒吧，喝了好多酒，用一种极具诱惑力的眼光环视全场。好多人上来搭腔："小姐，你好漂亮啊！"她喝了很多。当一个年纪可以做她爸爸的男人对她说"小姐，我送你回家吧"的时候她把手中的酒全泼在他的脸上，那个该死的

she **splashed** her drink onto his face. As the old man got ready to slap her, Ling showed up and saved Blue. I know all this because I was watching from a corner in the bar.

The 4th day

Today, she got up really early. After busying around all morning, she locked herself inside the bathroom. When her roommates opened the door, they were amazed. "So clean!"

The 5th day

She began studying. She had done very well in school before. However, when we got together, her grades **deteriorated**. It is good to focus on something else as it will improve recovery.

Three months later

She became president of the Student Union. She is becoming more and more able. She also becomes more open. Soon, she will need to prepare for graduate school.

One year later

There are many men beside her, many who are better than me. She never takes notice of them, but she gets along with Ling very well. There are rumors about them in school. She treats him like an elder brother, but rumor cannot be blocked.

Three years later

She is getting married. The

老头扬起他的手掌就要打下去的时候，凌来了，救了蓝。这一切我都知道，我就在酒吧的一个角落里看着。

第四天

今天她早早就起床了。忙忙碌碌了一上午，然后把自己关在浴室里好久，当舍友们踹门而入的时候都惊呼道："好干净啊！"

第五天

她开始学习了。其实她原来学习很好，我们在一起后，受我影响她的成绩也退步了，这也好，转移一下注意力，恢复得也快。

三个月后

她成了学生会主席，越来越能干，也开朗了不少，马上她就要考研了。

一年后

她身边的男生很多，比我优秀的也很多，可她根本没在意过，不过她和凌关系很好，校园里谣传他们的关系很暧昧。她只是把他当哥哥，可是流言是挡不住的。

三年后

她要结婚了，新郎是凌，

groom is Ling. She is writing wedding invitations. After she wrote one, two, and three…12th card, she bent over the desk and tears fell down uncontrollably. I stepped forward and saw that on all the invitations, the groom's name was mine.

I want to cry too, but ghost cannot cry. I do not have any tears.

Three years ago, when I was carrying her birthday cake crossing a street, a car crashed into me.

她在写结婚请帖，一张，两张，三张……写到第十二张的时候她哭了，趴在桌上，眼泪完全抑制不住。我上前一看，所有喜帖上的新郎名字写的都是我。

我也很想哭，可是鬼魂是不能哭的。我没有眼泪。

三年前，我过马路时遇上车祸，手里正提着要给她的生日蛋糕。

单词解析 Word Analysis

separate ['sepəreɪt] *v.* 分开；（使）分离；区分；隔开；（夫妻）分居；断绝关系 *adj.* 单独的；不同的；分开的，分离的

例 Each villa has a separate sitting-room.
每栋别墅都有一间独立的起居室。

beneath [bɪ'niːθ] *prep.* 在……的下方；（表示等级）低于；（表示状态）在……掩饰之下；（表示环境）在……影响之下 *adv.* 在下面；在底下

例 She could see the muscles of his shoulders beneath his T-shirt.
她可以看到他T恤衫下的肩部肌肉。

squirm [skwɜːrm] *v.* 局促不安；蠕动，扭动；难为情 *n.* 蠕动

例 He squirmed and wriggled and screeched when his father washed his face.
父亲给他洗脸时，他扭来扭去，尖声喊叫。

flirt [flɜːrt] *v.* 调情，打情骂俏；玩弄；轻率地对待

例 Dad's flirting with all the ladies, or they're all flirting with him, as usual.
和平常一样，爸爸在和所有的女士调情，或者说所有的女士都在和他调情。

splash [splæʃ] ⓥ 使（液体）溅起；（指液体）溅落 ⓝ（光、色等的）斑点；溅泼声；溅上的斑点；溅泼的量

例 A lot of people were in the water, swimming or simply splashing about.
水里有很多人，或在游泳或只是在戏水玩耍。

deteriorate [dɪ'tɪriəreɪt] ⓥ 使恶化；恶化，变坏

例 There are fears that the situation might deteriorate into full-scale war.
人们担心形势可能恶化而演变成一场全面战争。

语法知识点 *Grammar Points*

① Even though it was hard, I still had to let her go.

这句话中有两个结构 "even though" 和 "let...go"，分别表示 "即使" 和 "放手"。前者相当于 even if。

例 I occasionally procrastinate with writing, even though it is one of my favorite things to do.
偶尔我也会在写作上磨磨蹭蹭，即使它是我最喜欢做的事情之一。
Let go of things you can't change.
你改变不了的事情，就让它去吧。

② Her dorm mates were afraid to go in and comfort her.

这句话中有一个结构 "be afraid to do"，表示 "害怕做某事"。afraid 后面还可以加 of doing sth.。

例 Don't be afraid to ask for help if you need it.
倘若需要帮忙的话，尽管提出来（不必犹豫）。

③ As the old man got ready to slap her, Ling showed up and saved Blue.

这句话中有两个结构 "get ready to do" 和 "show up"，分别表示 "准备好做某事" 和 "出现"。get ready 后面可以用 for sth.。

例 Get ready to savor those bonito flakes.
准备好去品尝那些鲣鱼薄片。
The fingertips on the glass show up more clearly in the sunlight.
在阳光下玻璃杯上的指纹显得更清楚了。

④ **It is good to focus on something else as it will improve recovery.**

这句话中有一个结构"focus on"，表示"集中于"，相当于concentrate on。

例 Focus on one task until it's done, then move to the next.
集中精力对付一个任务，直到它完成才去做下一个任务。

⑤ **Soon, she will need to prepare for graduate school.**

这句话中有一个结构"prepare for"，表示"为……做好准备"。

例 I think that we should prepare for our future.
我想我们应该为将来做点准备。

⑥ **She never takes notice of them, but she gets along with Ling very well.**

这句话中有两个结构"take notice of"和"get along with"，分别表示"注意到，留心"和"与……和睦相处"。后者相当于get on with。

例 Will politicians take notice of such a model?
政治家会留意这个模式吗？

How do you get along with others?
你和别人相处得怎样？

经典名句 *Famous Classics*

1. I miss you when I am depressed, just as I miss the sunlight in winter; I miss you when I feel happy, just as I miss the shade in hot sun.
    我在忧愁时会想你，就像在冬天会想太阳；我在快乐时会想你，就像在骄阳下会想树荫。

2. Love means never having to say you're sorry.
    爱，意味着永不必说对不起。

3. When I met you I knew I would forever be by your side—forever be your partner and forever be your love.
    当我看到你时，我知道我会永远在你身边，做你的伴侣永远爱你。

4. I can't live without you by my side. No one can ever take your

place.
我不能没有你，没有人能代替你在我心中的位置。

5. There is no remedy for love but to love more.
治疗爱的创伤唯有加倍地去爱。

读书笔记

18 Love Between Two Dummies
两个哑巴的爱情

He was a **mute**. Although he could understand others' speech, he could not say his own actual feelings. She was his neighbor, a girl who was **bound by** a common destiny with her grandmother and always called him elder brother.

He really looked like an elder brother, leading her to go to school, accompanying her to play, and listening to her chirp with a smile.

He only used the hand **signal** conversing with her. She was able to read his every **expressions**. She knew how much he loved her when her brother fixed his eyes on her.

Afterwards, she finally completed the tests and went to college, **extremely** happy. He then started to go all out to make money, and then sent it continuously to her. She had not rejected.

Finally, she graduated, and started the work. Then she said firmly to him, "Elder brother, I must marry you!" He looked like only a frightened rabbit to **escape**, and was not willing to see her again no matter how she begged!

"Do you think I pity you? Do you think I **appreciate** you? No, I've fallen

他是个哑巴，虽然能听懂别人的话，却说不出自己的感受。她是他的邻居，一个从小和外婆相依为命的女孩。她总叫他哥哥。

他真像个哥哥，带她上学，伴她玩耍，含笑听她叽叽喳喳讲话。

他只用手势和她交谈，可她能读懂他的每一个表情。从哥哥注视她的目光里，她知道他有多么喜欢自己。

后来，她终于考上了大学，非常开心。他便开始拼命挣钱，然后源源不断地寄给她。她从来没有拒绝。

终于，她毕业了，参加了工作。然后，她坚定地对他说："哥哥，我要嫁给你！"他像只受惊的兔子逃掉了，再也不肯见她，无论她怎样哀求。

她说："你以为我同情你想报答你吗？不是，我十二岁就爱上了你。"可是。她得不到他的回答。

有一天，她突然住进了医院。他吓坏了，跑去看她。医生说，她喉咙里长了一颗瘤，

in love with you since I was 12." She said. But she could not **obtain** his reply.

One day, she had been **admitted to** the hospital suddenly. He was scared and ran to look for her. Doctor said, a tumor **destroyed** her **vocal cord**, and she would not possibly deliver the speech any more. On the hospital bed, her tearful eyes stared at him, and therefore they married.

After many years, nobody heard them to deliver a speech. They conversed with hands, pens and even looks. They shared joyful and sad stories. They loved each other so much that men and women all envied them. People said: "What a pair of happy mute husband and wife!"

Love could not prevent death's arrival. He abandoned her to leave first.

People feared she cannot undergo her lover's death and tried to comfort her. She looked at his **portrait** and opened the mouth to say suddenly that, "He finally left."

The truth was **revealed**...

虽然切除了，却破坏了声带，可能再也讲不了话了。病床上，她泪眼婆娑地注视着他，于是，他们结婚了。

很多年，没有人听他们讲过一句话。他们用手、用笔、用眼神交谈，分享喜悦和悲伤。他们成了所有相恋男女羡慕的对象。人们说："那是一对多么幸福的哑巴夫妻啊！"

爱情阻挡不了死神的降临，他撇下她一个人先走了。

人们怕她经受不住失去爱侣的打击来安慰她，这时，她收回注视他遗像的呆痴目光，突然开口说道："他还是走了。"

谎言被揭穿了……

单词解析 *Word Analysis*

mute [mjuːt] *adj.* 哑的；无声的；缄默的；（字母）不发音的 *n.* 哑巴；（乐器上的）弱音器 *v.* 减轻（声音）；使……柔和

例 He was mute, distant, and indifferent.
他一句话也不说，显得疏远而冷漠。

be bound by 束缚，限制

例 He is bound by affection.
他为爱情所束缚。

signal ['sɪgnəl] *n.* 信号，暗号；预兆，征象；动机；导火线 *v.* 向······发信号；用动作（手势）示意；以信号告知 *adj.* 显著的，优越的；暗号的，作信号用的

例 Kurdish leaders saw the visit as an important signal of support.
库尔德领导人将这次访问视作一种表示支持的重要信号。

escape [ɪ'skeɪp] *v.* 逃脱；逃离；躲过；泄露 *n.* 逃走；逃跑工具或方法；泄漏 *adj.* 使逃避困难的；使规避问题的

例 The man made his escape.
那个人逃跑了。

expression [ɪk'spreʃn] *n.* 表现，表示，表达；表情，脸色，态度

例 Laughter is one of the most infectious expressions of emotion.
笑是最具感染力的情感表达方式之一。

extremely [ɪk'stri:mli] *adv.* 极端地；非常，很

例 It condemned in extremely strong language what it called Britain's iniquitous campaign.
它言辞激烈地谴责了这场它所谓的英国极不公正的竞选活动。

appreciate [ə'priʃi,et] *v.* 欣赏；感激；领会；鉴别；（使）增值，涨价

例 Anyone can appreciate our music.
任何人都能欣赏我们的音乐。

obtain [əb'tein] *v.* 获得，得到；流行；买到，达到（目的）

例 Evans was trying to obtain a false passport and other documents.
埃文斯正试图取得一本假护照和其他证件。

be admitted to 承认；许可进入

例 Only Mimi's intimates were admitted to her boudoir.
只有米米的密友才被允许进入她的闺房。

destroy [dɪ'strɔɪ] ⦿ 杀死；破坏，摧毁；消灭，歼灭（敌人）；使失败

⑩ That's a sure recipe for destroying the economy and creating chaos.
那样做肯定会破坏经济、制造混乱。

vocal cord 声带；声襞

⑩ There're 8 pairs of consonants that differ only in the presence or lack of vocal cord vibration.
下面有八对辅音，它们的区别就在于声带是否振动。

portrait ['pɔːrtrət] ⦿ 肖像，肖像画；模型，标本；半身雕塑像；人物描写

⑩ Lucian Freud has been asked to paint a portrait of the Queen.
卢西恩·弗洛伊德已受邀为女王画肖像画。

reveal [rɪ'viːl] ⦿ 显露，揭露；泄露；[神]启示

⑩ Companies should be made to reveal more about their financial position.
应该要求公司使其财务状况更为透明化。

语法知识点 *Grammar Points*

① He only used the hand signal conversing with her.

这个句子中有一个结构 "converse with"，表示 "和……交谈"。相当于 talk with 以及 have a conversation with。

⑩ Don't feel that you must converse with everyone.
不要觉得你必须和每一个人交谈。

② He then started to go all out to make money, and then sent it continuously to her.

这个句子中有一个结构 "go all out to do"，表示 "鼓足干劲，全力以赴干某事"。

⑩ Now he is in trouble, so we should go all out to help him.
现在他遇到了麻烦，我们应该全力以赴去帮助他。

③ One day, she had been admitted to the hospital suddenly.

这个句子中有一个结构 "be admitted to do"，表示 "被……接纳，获准做某事"。

例 Mistakes must be admitted despite it hurts to do so.
犯了错误就应该承认，虽然这样做不好受。

经典名句 *Famous Classics*

1. No man or woman is worth your tears, and the one who is, won't make you cry.
没有人值得你流泪，值得你这么做的人不会让你哭泣。

2. If you fail, don't forget to learn your lesson.
如果你失败了，千万别忘了汲取教训。

3. Don't waste your time on a man/woman, who isn't willing to waste their time on you.
不要为那些不愿在你身上花费时间的人而浪费你的时间。

4. To the world you may be one person, but to one person you may be the world.
对于世界而言，你是一个人；但是对于某个人而言，你会是他的整个世界。

5. Never judge people by their appearance.
永远不要以貌取人。

读书笔记

----

19 Beautiful Love Story A
美丽的爱情故事 A

If only we'd never gone there, thought Alan. They were scrambling up the mountainside in the late afternoon heat. Alice was so **tanned** that she looked as if she had lived on the Mediterranean for months, while he, being fair, had turned a blotchy, peeling.

He looked up at the mountainside, the path twisting upwards towards the **cairn** cross, the white heat bleaching the rock. Why on earth couldn't they talk about it? Why couldn't he even accuse her?

He had thought it was going to be all right. But it was as if the heat had drained their love.

At home they had been so **blissfully** happy that he now realized it couldn't have lasted. She **came** to his school from the Midlands because her family had **split up**. As the only child, she lived with her father, and tried to look after him. Lonely, depressed and anxious, she had come to Alan to be healed. At least, that's what he liked to think. Had he **healed** her? No. Tom had, even though Alan loved her with all the passion. Now his hatred for both of them was as strong as his love.

艾伦心想：要是我们从未到过那个地方该多好。在炎热的后半晌，他们爬上山坡。爱丽丝被晒得黑黝黝的，看上去就像在地中海住过几个月似的；而原本细皮嫩肉的艾伦，这时身上已经像脱了一层皮似的，到处都是疤。

他抬头向山坡望去，只见小路盘旋而上通向那个圆锥形十字石碑，炽热的阳光将岩石晒得发白。他们究竟为什么不能谈那件事？他为什么连责骂她都不能呢？

他原以为一切都会好起来的，但好像酷热已经将他们的爱烤干。

在家时，他们曾是多么幸福。现在他意识到幸福不会再这样继续下去了。由于家庭破裂，她从内陆来到他的学校。作为独生女，她和她的父亲住在一起，尽力去照顾他。她孤独无依、无精打采、愁眉苦脸，经常到艾伦那里去寻求治愈。至少他乐意去这样想。他为她解忧了吗？没有。但汤姆却为她排忧解难，即使艾伦全

"Come on!" Alice had turned back to him, waving impatiently.

"Coming." Alan looked at his watch. Five. The **crickets** would start singing soon. He walked on, the sweat pouring into his eyes. He knew she had opened the bottle of **mineral** water. Would she let him catch up with her? An even greater **misery** seized him. It reminded him of the night he made himself drunk on the rough local wine his parents bought in the village. His heart had ached then, too, and his sense of loss had increased as he relived each minute of a day when Tom and Alice had seemed to draw closer and closer together.

He walked faster. Here, a few miles away on the bare mountainside, there was arid space, and the **olive** groves **clustered** in the cluttered-stone in the valleys below.

"Come on!"

"Coming."

Alan strode **doggedly** on, looking down at his red, peeling legs, thinking of Tom's strong, straight, and brown ones.

Suddenly he had turned to the corner by a stone shelter. He could see her waiting for him. If Tom were here, they would be together, mocking him, looking at each other, leaving him alone.

身心地爱着她。如今他对他们俩的恨就像他的爱一样强烈。

"跟上！"爱丽丝转身向他喊，不耐烦地挥着手。

"来了。"艾伦看了看手表。已经5点了。蛐蛐儿马上就要开始鸣唱了。他继续向上走，汗水源源不断地流到了眼里。他知道她已经打开那瓶矿泉水。她会让他跟上她吗？一种更大的痛苦折磨着他。这使他想起那天晚上他用父母亲从村里买的粗制的当地酒将自己灌醉的情景，那时他的心也在发痛。每当他想起爱丽丝和汤姆越来越亲近的时候，失落感就会剧增。

他走得越来越快。放眼望去，离那座山几里远的地方有一块空地，在山谷的乱石丛中生长着一小片橄榄林。

"跟上！"

"来了。"

艾伦仍顽强地大步前行，他低头看了一眼自己被晒红的、脱了皮的双腿，想起了汤姆强健挺拔的棕色的双腿。

突然，他拐到石头后面一块隐蔽的地方。他看到她正在等他。如果汤姆在这里的话，他们一定会站在一起嘲笑他，相互凝视，把他丢在一边。他拘谨地向前走，将注意力都集中在她

As he **strode** self-consciously on, Alan focused his mind on her.

"Where are we going to camp?" she was sitting on an outcrop, her slim body **supple** and salt-caked. Her legs were swinging and he longed to run his hands over them. Instead he imagined Tom doing that and hot, angry tears filled his eyes.

"Let's go." said Alan quickly.

"How far is it?" she asked. "I'm **whacked**."

"Half an hour."

"Can we eat them?" her voice was a little **plaintive**. Alan noticed with satisfaction that she was becoming dependent on him again. But he knew that once they were off the mountain she would be with Tom. For a crazy moment he imagined Alice with himself living in the mountain valley together. Forever. They were perhaps by some magical force that wouldn't let them leave.

The **monastery** was square-roofed, austere, with barrack windows. There were fish tanks at the back and a **terrace** on which the monks would walk around.

Their feet on the stones made the only sound. Santa Caterina was utterly still. A swift rose was soundlessly over the slate roof and the heat shimmered on the roughcast walls. They lay down, their **rucksack** still on their backs,

的身上。

"我们到哪去宿营？"她坐在一块突出的岩石上，身材修长而丰满。她的腿在那里晃来晃去，他真想将自己的手放在那上面滑动。然而他脑中浮现的却是汤姆那样做的情景。顿时，愤怒的热泪充满了他的眼睛。

"我们走吧。"艾伦飞快地说。

"还有多远？"她问，"我一点劲儿也没有了。"

"半小时吧。"

"我们能吃点东西吗？"她的声音有点儿伤感。艾伦心满意足，注意到她再一次变得依靠他。但他知道一旦他们离开这座大山，她就会和汤姆泡在一起。一时间，他竟荒唐地想象着爱丽丝和自己一起居住在这个山谷，直到永远。或许有某种魔力把他们困在这里，不让他们离开。

那座庙是方顶、木窗，十分简朴。庙后面有一些鱼缸，一个阳台，和尚可以在上面走来走去。

四周只有他们踏在石头上的声响，圣卡塔林纳万籁俱寂。一朵怒放的玫瑰在石板屋顶无声无息，亮光在粗糙的墙壁上闪烁。他们躺下来，越过

passing the water bottle, almost dozing.

Suddenly she sat up and looked him with surprising tenderness. Alan's black mood eased slightly.

"Have they all gone then?" asked Alice.

"Yes. I don't know when. A long time ago."

She was lying back, her eyes closed. He could talk to her now. They could both talk about the problem and solve it. They would reach each other. But he couldn't make the move.

"It would be terrible if it is pulled down." Alice said idly, her eyes still closed.

"It won't be."

"How do you know that?"

"They patch it up from time to time."

"Why don't they live here?"

"Don't know. Maybe it's too remote."

The desire to punish her had gone. But he daren't touch her. He daren't break the enchantment.

"The heat in the day. The cool evenings. It would be good to live like that."

水瓶，旅行包仍仍背在背后，他们几乎快要睡着了。

突然，她坐起来，用令人难以抗拒的温柔目光凝视着他。艾伦的难受情绪稍微得到了缓解。

"他们都已经走了吗？"爱丽丝问道。

"是的，我不知道是什么时候走的，走了好长时间了吧。"

她仰面躺着，双目紧闭。他现在可以和她谈了。他们俩谈谈那个问题，然后问题就迎刃而解了。他们彼此都能探到对方，但他不能动。

"如果庙被推倒，那将多么可怕。"爱丽丝懒懒地说，眼睛仍然闭着。

"不会的。"

"你怎么知道？"

"他们修补了一次又一次。"

"他们为什么不住在这里呢？"

"不知道，或许这里太偏远了吧。"

渐渐地，想惩罚她的欲望消失了，但他不敢触摸她，不敢轻易打破这令人着迷的时刻。

"白天热，夜里凉。住在这种地方会很不错的。"

单词解析 *Word Analysis*

tanned [tænd] *adj.* 被晒成棕褐色的；深褐色的；已鞣制的 *v.* 晒黑（tan 的过去分词）

例 His face is tanned.
他的脸晒黑了。

cairn [keən] *n.* 石冢，石堆纪念碑，堆石界标

例 A cairn and stone marker memorialize climber Scott Fischer, who died on Everest in 1996.
这是一个纪念在1996年葬身珠峰的登山者斯科特·菲舍尔的石冢。

blissfully ['blɪsfəlɪ] *adv.* 幸福地，充满喜悦地

例 He spent his blissfully carefree childhood in the countryside.
他在乡下度过了他无忧无虑的幸福童年。

split up 瓜分；劈成；（使）分成若干小部分；（使）断绝关系

例 Research suggests that children whose parents split up are more likely to drop out of high school.
研究表明，父母离异的孩子更容易从中学中途退学。

heal [hiːl] *v.* 恢复健康的状态；使恢复正常；使（某人）精神恢复健康

例 Within six weeks the bruising had gone, but it was six months before it all healed.
青瘀在6周内就消退了，但伤却是6个月后才全好了。

cricket ['krɪkɪt] *n.* 板球；蟋蟀；矮木凳 *v.* 打板球 *adj.* 公平的

例 During the summer term we would play cricket at the village ground.
在夏季学期，我们会在村里的空地上打板球。

mineral ['mɪnərəl] *n.* 矿物；矿物质；矿石；汽水 *adj.* 矿物的，似矿物的

例 The rock is rich in mineral salts.
该岩石中富含矿盐。

misery ['mɪzərɪ] *n.* 痛苦；不幸；穷困；悲惨的境遇

例 All that money brought nothing but sadness and misery and tragedy.

那笔钱带来的只有伤心、痛苦和悲剧。

olive [ˈɑːlɪv] *n.* 橄榄；橄榄色；橄榄树；油橄榄 *adj.* 橄榄色的；黄褐色的；淡褐色的；橄榄绿的

例 Olives look romantic on a hillside in Provence.
普罗旺斯一处山坡上的橄榄林呈现出一派浪漫风情。

cluster [ˈklʌstə] *n.* 群；丛；簇，串；[语言]辅音群 *v.* 丛生；群聚；使密集，使聚集

例 There's no town here, just a cluster of shops, cabins and motels at the side of the highway.
这儿没有城镇，只在公路边上有一片商店、小木屋和汽车旅馆。

strode [strəʊd] *v.* 大踏步走，跨过（stride的过去式）

例 He turned abruptly and strode off down the corridor.
他突然转身，沿走廊大步流星地走了。

doggedly [ˈdɒɡədlɪ] *adv.* 固执地，顽强地

例 They failed, but they doggedly kept at it.
他们失败了，但他们顽强地坚持了下来。

supple [ˈsʌpəl] *adj.* 灵活的；（身体）柔软的；易弯曲的；顺从的，巴结的

例 The leather is supple and sturdy enough to last for years.
该皮革柔软而结实，足以用上数年。

whack [wæk] *v.* 重击，使劲打；分配；击败；削减 *n.* 重击；一份儿；尝试；状况

例 You really have to whack the ball.
你真的需要猛击球才行。

plaintive [ˈplentɪv] *adj.* 悲哀的，哀怨的；哭诉的；可怜的；忧郁的

例 They lay on the firm sands, listening to the plaintive cry of the seagulls.
他们躺在硬实的沙地上，听着海鸥的哀鸣。

monastery ['mɑːnəsteri] *n.* 修道院，寺院；[复数]全体僧侣

例 The monastery is in a remote mountain pass.
那个修道院在一个偏远的山口中。

terrace ['terɪs] *n.* 阳台；台阶，阶地；柱廊，门廊 *v.* 把（如山坡或坡地）修成梯田；给（如房屋）建阳台

例 The idea of building a roof terrace was also foiled by the planning authorities.
建造一个带棚阳台的想法也被规划局否决了。

rucksack ['rʌkˌsæk,'rʊk-] *n.* 帆布背包

例 My rucksack was too big for the luggage rack.
我的背包太大了，行李架上放不下。

语法知识点 *Grammar Points*

① **Alice was so tanned that she looked as if she had lived on the Mediterranean for months, while he, being fair, had turned a blotchy, peeling.**

这个句子中有一个结构"as if"，表示"好像，犹如，好似"。后面一般接虚拟语气。

例 You'll feel as if you were at home while here.
到这儿就好像到了自己家一样。

② **As the only child, she lived with her father, and tried to look after him. Lonely, depressed, anxious, she had come to Alan to be healed.**

这个句子中有两个结构"look after"和"come to"，分别表示"照顾"和"到达，想起"。前者相当于take care of。

例 It's her duty to look after her aunt.
照顾她姨妈是她分内的事。

Let me come at once, or at once come to me!
让我立刻到你那儿去吧，或者你立刻到我这儿来！

③ It reminded him of the night he made himself drunk on the rough local wine his parents bought in the village.

这个句子中有一个结构 "remind sb. of"，表示"提醒，使想起"。

例 Alas! You only remind me of what I have lost.
唉……你只是使我想起我所失去的一切。

经典名句 *Famous Classics*

1. Don't believe in waiting, because you have to spend a lot of time seeing all the aspects.
别相信等待，因为你要耗费很多时间来看清所有的面。

2. Loving a person who does not love you is like holding a cactus. The closer you hold, the more hurt you are.
爱一个不爱你的人就像抱着一颗仙人掌，抱得越紧，伤得越重。

3. I don't think I have a strong enough heart to forgive your betrayal again and again.
我想我没有一颗足够强大的心脏，来原谅你再三的背叛。

4. Never think it's easy to be perfunctory; it will make you lose what you get.
永远别以为敷衍很简单，它会让你把得到的都失去。

5. Anyone who wants to rely on me to maintain the relationship, I'll let you go.
任何要靠我来主动维持关系的人，我坦然送你走。

读书笔记

20 Beautiful Love Story B
美丽的爱情故事 B

"Live here?"

"Could we ever get permission?"

"I don't know."

"Just to see what it was like. I mean," she half sat up. "Can we get inside?" she ran a finger gently down his peeling cheek.

Alan was taken aback but then he became aware that the crickets had started. How long had they been singing? He wondered. "Let's go and see."

They **tramped** round but as Alan already knew, there was no way in. In the end they came back and he lit a fire at the side of a small stone building. Other campers had obviously used the space and there were black marks on the walls.

He cooked supper, using half a precious bottle of water. The **intimacy** was still there but the talking was at an end. Alan could hardly contain his rising excitement. They had night together. Anything could happen.

Alan suddenly realized what he had to do. After supper, in the glow of the scented mountain twilight, he made coffee and they sat in silence. Darkness

"住在这里？"

"我们可以住这儿吗？"

"不知道。"

"先看看这里怎么样，我是说，"她半坐了起来。"我们能进去吗？"她将一根手指轻轻地放在他脱皮的脸颊上。

他吃了一惊，随后意识到蛐蛐儿的鸣叫声已经响起。他不知道它们已经鸣唱了多长时间。"让我们去看看吧。"

他们绕过去，但正如艾伦所料，无路可进。最后，他们又原路返回，在一座小型石头建筑旁生了一堆火。显然，其他野营的人也曾使用过这个地方，墙壁上还留有黑色的痕迹。

他做晚饭用去了半瓶珍贵的水。亲密关系依旧存在，但他们已经无话可说。艾伦按捺不住正在膨胀的冲动。他们一起度过这个夜晚，任何事情都可能会发生。

艾伦突然意识到他必须得做些什么了。晚饭后，在芳香弥漫的大山的幽光中，他煮了咖啡，他们默默地坐在一起。夜幕

came slowly; the volume of the crickets seemed to increase. Still he had made no moves.

She was lying in front of the fire, her body almost glowing. Alan reached out a hand and temporarily she took it. Then Alice yawned and stretched. "I'm turning in now." she said.

"More coffee?" asked Alan miserably.

She kissed him on the forehead. "No, thanks."

Had he ever loved his brother Tom? He must have done sometime. Certainly he had always been jealous of him as a child. He the **introvert**; Tom the extrovert. Alan thought about his introverted personality. He could see quite clearly how he had failed so dismally with Alice and how Tom had taken over so easily. Tom was what she wanted. She didn't want what he had.

Gloomily, Alan climbed into the sleeping bag and **drifted** off to sleep. Beside him Alice slept, her breathing seeming to keep in time with the insistent beat of crickets.

Alan dreamt. The crickets had stopped. There was a slight breeze and the luminous hand of his watch registered just after two. Her sleeping bag was empty; Alice had gone. For a while he just couldn't believe it. He sat up and felt the dark walls of Santa

慢慢地降临；蛐蛐儿好像升高了音量。可他仍没有行动。

她躺在火堆前，身上闪闪发光。艾伦伸出一只手，她握了一下他的手，马上又放开了。接着，爱丽丝打哈欠，伸了个懒腰。"我现在要睡觉了。"她说。

"再来点咖啡？"艾伦痛苦地问道。

她在他的前额上吻了吻。"不用了，谢谢。"

他爱他的弟弟汤姆吗？他肯定爱过，年幼时，他总是嫉妒他弟弟。他们俩一个内向，一个外向。艾伦想着自己内向的性格。他十分清楚自己如何在爱丽丝身上败得这么惨，而汤姆又是如何轻而易举成了赢家。汤姆正是她需要的那种人，她并不需要他这种人。

艾伦闷闷不乐地钻进自己的睡袋，渐渐地进入了梦乡。躺在他身旁的爱丽丝也睡着了，她的呼吸声和蛐蛐儿的鸣叫声此起彼伏。

艾伦做了一个梦。蛐蛐声都停止了。一阵微风拂过，他手表上的夜光针刚过了两点。爱丽丝的睡袋空了，她已经走了。好一阵子，他都无法相信这个事实。他坐起来，感到圣卡塔林纳黑黢黢的墙壁将他团

Caterina close in on him.

Then he was on the mountainside, stumbling blindly up the mountain path, hearing their laughter. Softly he crept up on them until he could see their bodies entwined. Alan's anger rose to fever pitch and he rushed towards them. They fell apart. He sobbed as he had never sobbed since he was a child.

She woke him anxiously shaking at his sunburnt shoulders.

"What's the matter?" she kept asking over and over again. "Alan, what's wrong?"

He stared up at her, blinking in the glow of the dying camp fire.

"Nothing," he said automatically, "Nothing really."

"But..."

"Just a bad dream, that's all."

"You were crying." Her voice was soft, tender, just like she used to be.

Alan turned over in his sleeping bag. "I'm fine." he said, "Let's get some sleep."

Alan woke with the early-morning sun gently warming his face. He sat up, his head **muzzy** with the dream, his cheeks salty, tear-stained. "You were crying." Her voice came back to him and he **winced**. Alice had felt sorry for him and he instantly felt smothered. He broke into a sweat of agony and

团围住了。

随后，他来到山边，踉踉跄跄地沿着山路盲目前行。听见他们的朗朗笑声。他轻轻地爬过去，看到两个人的身体紧紧地贴在一块。他感到痛苦万分，怒不可遏地冲向他们。他们猛地分开了。他低声啜泣，尽管他从孩提起就从来没有哭过。

她焦急地摇着他被太阳晒黑的肩膀，唤醒了他。

"发生了什么事？"她一遍又一遍地问，"艾伦，怎么了？"

他抬眼盯着她，在篝火的余光中眨着眼睛。

"没什么，"他不由自主地说，"真的没什么。"

"可是……"

"只是一个噩梦，仅此而已。"

"你刚才在哭。"她的声音像过去那样温柔和气。

艾伦在睡袋里翻了一下身，背对着她说："我很好，再睡一会儿吧！"

艾伦醒来时，晨光暖暖地照在他的脸上。他满脸泪痕，咸咸的。他坐起来，脑海里还懵懵懂懂地萦绕着那个梦。"你刚才在哭。"她的声音又传了过来。他退缩了一下。爱丽丝已经

apprehension. How could he ever open up a discussion with her now?

He looked cautiously round her sleeping bag. It was empty and Alan froze. Then, gradually, he relaxed. It was just after eight and she had probably gone to find a place used as the loo. He waited, calmly and gloomily, and then anxiously as she did not appear. Hurriedly Alan struggled out of his sleeping bag and began to search the grounds of the monastery. But there was no sign of her at all.

Panic set in as Alan scoured the grounds again and drew a blank for the second time. It was becoming increasingly obvious that she had walked out on him and was probably climbing down to Tom. But rather than feeling angry, Alan simply felt desolate. She hadn't even left him a note. He went over and touched the inside of her sleeping bag. It felt cold.

Surely she wouldn't find her way back alone. Alan began to search again, this time through the tangled thickets of what might have been a herb garden. Something caught his eye. Lying on the ground was a small, shiny object. It was Alice's **bracelet**.

Suddenly real fear clutched at him: someone must had come and abducted her. Or had Tom come to find her? But

感到对不起他了。他立即感到很压抑。由于巨大的悲痛和忧伤，猛地出了一身冷汗。现在他该怎样和她谈谈呢？

他小心翼翼地看了看她的睡袋，睡袋已经空了。艾伦一下子僵住了。随后，他渐渐放松。现在刚过8点，她也许是找地方方便去了。他平静又忧郁地等待着，而后还是不见她回来，就心急火燎起来。艾伦慌忙从睡袋里挣扎出来，开始在寺院里四处寻找。但皆无她的踪迹。

当艾伦再次四处寻找仍然一无所获时，他顿感恐慌，显然她已不辞而别，很可能是下山找汤姆去了。艾伦感到，与其说是生气，倒不如说是孤独。她甚至连一张纸条也没有给他留下。他走过去将手伸进她的睡袋，里面冷冰冰的。

她肯定无法独自找到回路。艾伦又开始找起来，这一次去到杂草丛生的灌木丛中。某个东西引起了他的注意。躺在地上的是一个小小的、光亮的东西，那是爱丽丝的手镯。

突然，一种真正的恐惧袭上他的心头：一定是有人拐走了她？或者是汤姆来找她的？可是，手镯又怎么解释呢？

"拜托，上帝，"艾伦

the bracelet?

"Please God." Alan **muttered**, "Let her be safe." "Why hadn't he looked after her? Why hadn't he been able to reassure her? Alan now realized how he had locked himself into his own shell of rejection and jealousy. Tom no longer seemed a threat. All Alan wanted was Alice, and if only he could find her they would talk and talk and talk."

For the fourth time he began to search the grounds, the bracelet in his hands. Then in a crevice on the broken stones of the terrace, he saw something bright and beady. Alice's ring. And he knew how tight on her finger it was. Sweat ran down Alan's face.

"Alice." he cried out, "Alice!" No response. Alan began to run.

It was only when he was back at the front door of the monastery that he realized there was one place he had not been to. His heart **thumping** and his throat dry, he went down the steps.

Now he ran eagerly forward, pushing his way through the foliage. He gave a gasp of relief. She was there, lying on the pine needles.

"Alice."

She woke slowly, sleepily, stretching in the sun. "Sorry, I fell asleep."

"Where the hell have you been?"

喃喃道，"保佑她平安。"为什么他没有照顾她？为什么也没有安慰她？现在艾伦才意识到他以前是如何将自己锁进一个妒忌和沮丧的空壳里。汤姆现在看起来似乎不再是一种威胁。艾伦满脑子想的都是爱丽丝，只要能找到她，他们就可以倾心长谈。

他手里拿着那只手镯开始第四次寻找，随后在一排房屋堆砌的石头缝里他看见一件东西在发光——是爱丽丝的戒指。而且他知道那是紧紧地戴在她的手上的。艾伦的汗从脸上流了下来。

"爱丽丝，"他喊道，"爱丽丝！"没有回应。艾伦开始跑了起来。

正当他惊恐地返回到那座庙的前门时，他意识到还有一个地方他没有去找。他走下台阶，心怦怦直跳，嗓子发干。

他急不可待地跑上前，推开树叶，看到她在那里，躺在松叶上，心里松了一口气。

"爱丽丝。"

她慢慢地醒来了，睡眼惺忪地在太阳下伸伸懒腰。"对不起，我睡着了。"

"你究竟到哪里去了？"

"我出去走了走，对不起。"

"I went for a walk." "I'm sorry."

"That's not enough."

"I laid a trail."

"You did what?" He was **outraged**.

"I wanted you to find me."

"I was terrified...I thought..."

"I'm sorry." She stood up, "I suppose I wanted to frighten you."

"Why?" He barked at her.

She looked away again. "I didn't think you wanted me any more."

"Wanted you?"

"You haven't spoken to me. You seemed so cold. Indifferent somehow."

"But it's you who were indifferent."

She looked genuinely amazed. "I don't know what you're talking about."

"I thought you wanted Tom; didn't want to be with me." his voice broke.

"I thought you found him...more fun."

"Him? oh, he's a baby. I was lonely, I suppose. You seemed so fed up with me. I didn't realize it would...oh, Alan." She got up and drew him to her, kissing him so hard on the lips. "You are such a bloody fool. I love you-don't you know?"

"Why did you come here?" he asked.

"I was wandering about. I couldn't sleep. Look—" she **knelt** down and stared at the Latin inscription on the two

"说'对不起'就够了？"

"我有一路留记号的。"

"你留了什么？"他怒气冲冲地说。

"我想让你找到我。"

"我当时很害怕……我还以为……"

"对不起，"她站起来，"我原本只是想吓唬吓唬你的。"

"为什么？"他大声问道。

她又一次转移了目光，"我还以为你不要我了呢。"

"要你？"

"你话都不和我说，似乎很冷淡的样子，某种程度上可以说是无动于衷了。"

"可无动于衷的是你。"

她看上去真的很吃惊。"我真不知道你在说什么。"

"我还以为你想要汤姆，不想和我在一块。"他的声音沙哑了。

"我还以为你找他……开心去了呢。"

"他？噢，他还是一个小毛孩子。我觉得孤独。你好像很烦我。我没有意识到那么……噢，艾伦。"她站起来，将他拉向自己，深深地吻起了他的嘴唇。"你真是个大傻瓜。我爱你——难道你不知道吗？"

"你怎么来到这了？"他问道。

solitary graves. "Who are they?" she asked.

"I don't know. I've often wondered. Dom Carols Fuenta—he's definitely a monk. But the odd thing is that he's buried alongside a woman." He paused and then went on. "Maria Degardes. He was buried in 1892. She was in 1894."

"Were they lovers?"

"I used to make up stories that they were."

"I was just thinking. A silly thought. I expect you'll laugh."

"Try me."

"Suppose we lived here for the rest of our lives and when we died we were buried here. But in one grave. Together."

Alan took Alice's face in his hands and kissed her on the lips.

"我就是随便走走，睡不着。瞧——"她跪下来，盯着前面两座孤坟的拉丁碑文问道："他们是什么人？"

"我不知道。我也总是想知道。多姆·卡罗斯·福恩塔——他肯定是一个和尚。但奇怪的是，他和一个女人葬在一起。"他暂停了一下，然后接着说道："玛丽姬·德拉斯。他葬于1892年，而她葬于1894年。"

"他们是情人吗？"

"我过去经常编故事设定他们是。"

"我刚才在想……是一个愚蠢的想法，我想你会笑我的。"

"说说看。"

"假如我们今后生活在这里，我们死后就埋在这里，但要合葬在一块。"

艾伦用双手捧起爱丽丝的脸，亲吻她的嘴唇。

单词解析 *Word Analysis*

tramp [træmp] *v.* 步行；踩；踏；漂泊；践踏 *n.* 流浪汉；妓女；游民；徒步旅行，远足

例 She spent all day yesterday tramping the streets, gathering evidence.
她昨天一整天都在街上四处奔走，搜集证据。

intimacy ['ɪntəməsi] *n.* 亲密；亲近；亲昵的言行；性行为

例 Her sunburn made intimacy too painful.
她的皮肤晒伤了，使得想要亲热一下都变得很痛苦。

introvert ['ɪntrəvɜːrt] *n.* 性格内向的人

例 The music students here are a very introvert lot.
这里学音乐的学生都非常不爱交际。

gloomily ['gluːməlɪ] *adv.* 忧郁地；阴郁地；阴暗地；阴沉地

例 We are in trouble, he said gloomily.
我们遇上了麻烦，他沮丧地说道。

drift [drɪft] *v.* 漂泊；流动；随意移动；浮现 *n.* 漂移，偏移；趋势，动向；大意；放任自流

例 We proceeded to drift on up the river.
我们继续向河流的上游漂流。

muzzy ['mʌzi] *adj.* 迷糊的；昏头昏脑的；模糊的；不清晰的

例 After a couple of whiskies my head felt all muzzy.
我喝了两杯威士忌，就昏头昏脑的了。

wince [wɪns] *v.* 赶紧避开；畏缩，退避 *n.* （由于疼痛、吃惊等）畏缩，退缩

例 Every time he put any weight on his left leg he winced in pain.
只要左腿一受力，他就会疼得龇牙咧嘴。

bracelet ['breslɪt] *n.* 手镯；手铐

例 He picked the bracelet up for me.
他帮我把手镯捡了起来。

mutter ['mʌtər] *v.* 轻声低语，咕哝地抱怨；含糊地说；自言自语地说 *n.* 咕哝；小声低语，小声抱怨；怨言

例 "God knows what's happening in that madman's mind," she muttered.
她咕哝着："天知道那个疯子在想什么。"

thumping ['θʌmpɪŋ] *adj.* 重击的；重大的，巨大的；尺码大的；极好的 *adv.* 极端地；非常地 *v.* 重击(thump的现在分词)；狠打；怦怦地跳；全力支持

例 The Right has a thumping majority.
右派占绝大多数。

outrage ['aʊtreɪdʒ] v 引起……的义愤，激怒；辱，强奸；虐待，迫害；违反

例 Many people have been outraged by some of the things that have been said.
其中的一些言论激怒了很多人。

knelt [nɛlt] v 跪（kneel的过去式和过去分词）

例 She knelt and brushed her lips softly across Michael's cheek.
她跪了下来，轻吻迈克尔的脸颊。

语法知识点 *Grammar Points*

① **Alan was taken aback but then he became aware that the crickets had started.**

这个句子中有一个结构 "be taken aback"，表示"吃了一惊，吓了一跳"。

例 You should not be taken aback with some issues that might put you off at first reading.
在你第一次展卷阅读时，不要惊讶于那些困扰你的问题。

② **She was lying in front of the fire, her body almost glowing.**

这个句子中有一个结构 "in front of"，表示"在……前面"。注意区分in front of 和 in the front of。后者是指在内部的前面，in front of 表示在外部的前面。如in front of the desk 表示在桌子的前面；in the front of the house 表示在房间里的前面。

例 Our school is in front of the factory.
我们的学校就在那个工厂的前面。

③ **Certainly he had always been jealous of him as a child.**

这个句子中有一个结构 "be jealous of sb."，表示"嫉妒"。相当于 envy sb.。

例 So how can you admit you're jealous of your friend?
所以你怎么可以允许自己妒忌自己的朋友呢？

④ **Alice had felt sorry for him and he instantly felt smothered.**

这个句子中有一个结构 "fell sorry for"，表示"为……感到可惜/难过"。

例 Before long, his son became fond of riding. One day he fell from a horse and broke his leg. Again, his neighbors all felt sorry for him.

没多久，塞翁的儿子就喜欢上了骑马。一天他从马上掉了下来，摔断了腿。邻居们都替塞翁难过。

⑤ **Hurriedly Alan struggled out of his sleeping bag and began to search the grounds of the monastery.**

这个句子中有一个结构 "begin to do sth."，表示"开始做某事"。相当于 start to do sth.。begin 和 start 后面也可以直接加 doing。

例 In autumn the days begin to draw in.
到了秋天，白天开始渐渐短起来。

经典名句 *Famous Classics*

1. Do not be an excellent person, but be an irreplaceable person.
不要做一个单纯优秀的人，而要做一个不可替代的人。

2. I would rather have a friend who can understand my tears, and not a group of people who only know my smiles.
宁愿要一个能懂我眼泪的朋友，也不要一群只懂我笑容的人。

3. Don't you know I'm strong? You don't know that I am strong enough to do all.
你不知道我很强大吗？你不知道我强大到所向披靡吗？

4. Your eyes are like a star that illuminates my life with the night.
你的眼睛像一颗恒星，撑着黑夜照亮我的生命。

5. When you make up your mind to persist until you cannot, you are qualified to be capricious.
当你下定决心无论如何都要坚持到最后一秒，那样才有资格任性。

21 Who You Love
你爱的是谁

Jim was waiting for a girl whose heart he knew, but whose face he didn't, the girl with the rose.

"You'll **recognize** me," she wrote, "by the red rose I'll be wearing on my **lapel**." So he was looking for the girl with the red rose.

A young woman in a green suit was coming toward him, her figure long and slim and her eyes were blue as flowers. Almost **uncontrollably** he made one step closer to her, and just at this moment he saw Hollis Maynell a woman well past 40. The girl was walking quickly away. He felt as though he was split in two, so keen was his desire to follow her, and yet so deep was his longing for the woman whose spirit had truly **companioned** him and upheld his own.

He did not **hesitate**. He squared his shoulders and said, "I'm John, and you must be Miss Maynell. I am so glad you could meet me; may I take you to dinner?"

The woman smiled, "I don't know what this is about, son," she answered, "but the young lady in the green suit begged me to wear this rose on my coat.

吉姆正在等一个手拿玫瑰花的女孩，他和她互相熟悉却素未谋面。

"你会认出我的，"她写道，"我会把一朵红玫瑰别在衣领上。"所以他就在车站寻找那位带着红玫瑰的女孩。

一位身穿绿色衣服的年轻女子向他走来，她身材修长而苗条，眼睛蓝蓝的，美如鲜花。他不由自主地向她靠近了一步。就在这时，他看见了哈里斯·玛尼尔——一位年过四十的女人。女孩很快地走开了。他感觉自己好像被分裂成了两半——他是多么强烈地想跟随那位年轻女子，然而又是如此深切地向往这位在心灵上陪伴他、鼓舞他的女人。

他没有迟疑，挺起胸膛，说道："我是约翰，你一定是玛尼尔小姐吧。我很高兴认识你，我能请你吃饭吗？"

她笑了笑，回答说："孩子，我不知道这是怎么回事，但是那位穿绿衣的年轻女子请求我把这朵玫瑰别在我的外套上面。她说如果你邀请我吃饭

And she said if you were to ask me out to dinner, I should tell you that she is waiting for you in the restaurant across the street. She said it was some kind of test!"

It's not difficult to admire Miss Maynell's wisdom. The true nature of a heart is seen in it's response to the unattractive.

的话，我就告诉你她在马路对面的餐厅等你。她说这是对你的考验！"

玛尼尔小姐的智慧让人敬佩。一个人对那些平淡无奇的事物的表现恰恰反映出他内心的本质。

单词解析 *Word Analysis*

recognize ['rɛkəg,naɪz] *v.* 承认；识别；认出；确认

例 The receptionist recognized him at once.
接待员一眼就认出他了。

lapel [lə'pɛl] *n.* （西服上衣或夹克的）翻领

例 The badge sits on the lapel of his suit.
徽章佩戴在他西服的翻领上。

uncontrollably [,ʌnkən'trəuləbli] *adv.* 无法控制地

例 You feel so cold that your body starts to shake, not very much but uncontrollably.
你觉得如此冷以至于你的身体开始颤抖，不是很严重但不可控制。

companion [kəm'pænjən] *n.* 同伴；同甘共苦的伙伴 *v.* 陪伴；同行

例 She was a wonderful companion and her generosity to me was entirely selfless.
她是一个极好的伴侣，她对我慷慨大方，一心只为我着想。

hesitate ['hezɪteɪt] *v.* 犹豫，踌躇；不愿；支吾；停顿；对……犹豫；不情愿

例 The telephone rang. Catherine hesitated, debating whether to answer it.
电话响了。凯瑟琳犹豫了一下要不要去接。

语法知识点 *Grammar Points*

① **Jim was waiting for a girl whose heart he knew, but whose face he didn't, the girl with the rose.**

这个句子中有一个结构"wait for"，表示"等待"，相当于await。

 Why not just wait for that to happen?
为什么不等待那种情况发生？

② **So he was looking for the girl with the red rose.**

这个句子中有一个结构"look for"，表示"寻找"。look for和find不一样，前者是寻找的过程，后者是找到的结果。

 What signs should physicians look for?
医师应该寻找什么样的迹象？

③ **He felt as though he was split in two, so keen was his desire to follow her, and yet so deep was his longing for the woman whose spirit had truly companioned him and upheld his own.**

这个句子中有一个结构"as though"，表示"好像，仿佛"。相当于as if。

 It sounds as though you enjoyed Peru.
听起来好像你喜欢秘鲁。

④ **The woman smiled, "I don't know what this is about, son," she answered, "but the young lady in the green suit begged me to wear this rose on my coat."**

这个句子中有一个结构"beg sb. to do"，表示"祈求某人干某事"。同义词组还有implore sb. to do sth.。

 He begged her to stay, but she simply laughed and put her bags in the car.
他祈求她留下，但是她只是笑笑把包放进了车里。

⑤ **The true nature of a heart is seen in it's response to the unattractive.**

这个句子中有一个结构"the response to sth."，表示"对……的反应"。

 They have made generous response to the appeals for funds.
他们对募集资金的呼吁做出了慷慨的响应。

经典名句 *Famous Classics*

1. Don't cry because it is over; smile because it happened.
不要因为结束而哭泣，微笑吧，为你曾经拥有。

2. True love does not come by finding the perfect person, but by learning to see an imperfect person perfectly.
获得真爱不是靠寻觅完美之人，而是学会把不完美之人看得完美。

3. Never let a problem to be solved become more important than a person to be loved.
决不让悬而未决的问题阻挡我们去爱应爱之人。

4. To forgive is not to forget, nor remit, but let it go.
原谅并不代表忘记，也不代表赦免，而是放自己一条生路。

5. Therefore, if you desire love, try to realize that the only way to get love is by giving love, that the more you give, the more you get.
如果你渴望爱，你需意识到得到爱的唯一方法就是付出爱，你付出的越多，得到的就越多。

读书笔记

22 Chance
偶然

I am a cloud in the sky,

A chance **shadow** on the **wave** of your heart.

Don't be surprised,

Or too **elated**.

In an **instant** I shall **vanish** without trace.

We meet on the sea in a dark night.

You on your way, I on mine.

Remember if you will,

Or, better still, forget,

The light **exchanged** in this **encounter**.

我是天空中的一片云，

偶尔投影在你的心上。

你不必讶异，

也无须欢喜。

刹那间，我将消失无影踪，

你我相逢在黑夜的海上，

你我有着自己的方向。

你记得也好，

又或最好忘掉，

在这交汇时互放的光芒。

单词解析 *Word Analysis*

shadow [ˈʃædəʊ] *n.* 阴影；影子；鬼，幽灵；隐蔽处 *v.* 投阴影于；使朦胧；跟踪，尾随；预示；渐变；阴沉 *adj.* 阴影的；影子内阁的

例 It was without a shadow of a doubt that this was the best we've played.

毫无疑问这是我们表现最出彩的一次。

wave [weɪv] *n.* 挥手；波浪，波动；汹涌的行动（或思想）态势 *v.*（一端固定地）飘扬；挥手指引；挥手表示；挥舞

例 Tina waved him away with a show of irritation.

缇娜恼火地挥手让他离开。

elated [ɪ'leɪtɪd] *adj.* 兴高采烈的，得意洋洋的 *v.* 使兴奋

例 I was elated that my second heart bypass had been successful.
第二次心脏搭桥手术成功了，我很高兴。

instant ['ɪnstənt] *n.* 瞬间，顷刻；此刻；当月；速食食品，即溶饮料 *adj.* 立即的；迫切的；正在考虑的，目前的；即食的

例 For an instant, Catherine was tempted to flee.
有那么一会儿，凯瑟琳很想逃跑。

vanish ['vænɪʃ] *v.* 消失；突然不见；消亡，消灭；[数]化为零；使消失，使不见 *n.* [语音学]消失音，弱化音

例 Anne vanished from outside her home last Wednesday.
安妮上周三突然在家门外失踪了。

exchange [ɪks'tʃendʒ] *n.* 交换；交易所；交易；兑换（率）*v.* 兑换；交换，调换

例 I'm going to go on an exchange visit to Paris.
我将到巴黎交流参观。

encounter [ɛn'kaʊntɚ] *v.* 遭遇；不期而遇；对抗 *n.* 相遇，碰见；遭遇战；对决，冲突

例 Did you encounter anyone in the building?
你在大楼里遇到谁了吗？

语法知识点 *Grammar Points*

① In an instant I shall vanish without trace.

这个句子中有一个结构 in an instant 和 without trace，分别表示"瞬间，马上"和"了无痕迹"。前者相当于 at once。

例 They forgot all their fears and all their miseries in an instant.
他们马上忘记了一切恐惧和痛苦。

He seems to have vanished without trace.
他似乎消失得无影无踪。

② You on your way, I on mine.

这个句子是一个省略句。还原句子应该是：

You are on your way; I am on my way.

经典名句 *Famous Classics*

1. Hot love is soon cold.
   热烈的爱冷淡得快。

2. When you are happy, do not lose the virtue that makes you happy.
   当你幸福的时候，切勿丧失使你幸福的德行。

3. Love needs a thin layer of sadness, needs a little jealousy, doubt, and dramatic game.
   爱情需要薄薄的一层忧伤，需要一点点嫉妒、疑虑、戏剧性的游戏。

4. The object of your marriage is that you feel the most suitable for you in the most vulnerable times.
   你结婚的对象应是你在最脆弱时觉得最适合你的人。

读书笔记

23 *Discuss Love* Written by Bacon
培根《论爱情》

The stage is more beholding to love, than the life of man. For as to the stage, love is ever matter of comedies, and now and then of tragedies; but in life it does much mischief; sometimes like a **siren**, sometimes like a **fury**.

You may observe that among all the great and worthy persons, **whereof** the memory remained, either ancient or recent, there is not one that **hath** been transported to the mad degree of love: which shows that great spirits, and great business, do keep out this weak passion. You must except, nevertheless, Marcus Antonius, the half partner of the empire of Rome, and Appius Claudius, the decemvir and lawgiver; whereof the former was indeed a voluptuous man, and inordinate; but the latter was an austere and wise man; and therefore it seems though rarely that love can find entrance, not only into an open heart, but also into a heart well **fortified**, if watch be not well kept.

It is a poor saying of Epicurus: "Satis **magnum** alter alteri theatrum sumus"; as if man, made for the **contemplation** of heaven, and all noble objects, should do nothing but kneel

舞台上的爱情要比生活中的爱情美好得多。在舞台上，爱情永远都是喜剧的题材，也不时成为悲剧的内容。但在人生中，爱情时而如艳女，时而如泼妇，惹是生非，招灾致祸。

值得注意的是，所有古今伟大而尊贵的人物，只要是我们还记得的，还没有一个会在爱情中被诱至头脑发昏的程度，可见伟大的人物和伟大的事业的确可与这种孱弱之情毫不沾边。然而，有两个必须视为例外的人，一是曾为罗马帝国两个合伙统治者之一的马库斯·安东尼奥斯，还有就是作为十大执政官之一和拟订法典的阿皮尔斯·克劳迪亚斯。前者确是一个好色之徒，放纵无度；但后者却是一个严肃而多谋的人。所以，虽然不多见，但看起来，爱情不但会对不设防之心长驱直入，即使对严阵以待之心，也照样随进随驻，如果把守稍有松弛的话。

伊壁鸠鲁说过一句蹩脚的话，"我们彼此都是值得对方观赏的"，好像生来即向往天

before a little idol, and make himself a subject, though not of the mouth as beasts are, yet of the eye; which was given him for higher purposes.

It is a strange thing, to note the excess of this passion, and how it braves the nature, and value of things, by this; that the speaking in a perpetual hyperbole, is comely in nothing but in love. Neither is it merely in the phrase; for whereas it hath been well said, that the arch-flatterer, with whom all the petty flatterers have intelligence, is a man's self; certainly the lover is more. For there was never proud man thought so **absurdly** well of himself, as the lover **doth** of the person loved; and therefore it was well said: "That it is impossible to love, and to be wise." Neither doth this weakness appear to others only, and not to the party loved; but to the loved most of all, except the love be reciprocal.

For it is a true rule, that love is ever rewarded, either with the **reciprocal**, or with an inward and secret contempt. By how much the more, men ought to beware of this passion, which lose not only other things, but itself! As for the other losses, the poet's relation doth well figure them: that the person who preferred Helena, quitted the gifts of Juno and Pallas. For whosoever esteeme too much of amorous affection, quitte

堂及一切崇高事物的人类不该干别的，只应跪在一个小偶像面前，自己任由对方眼目所奴役，虽然还不至于如畜生一般为胃口所奴役，但上帝赐给人眼目本是为了更崇高之目的。

看到这种情欲之放纵，极其不顾事情里果和意义就而肆意妄为的结果，真是触目惊心。就此而言，浮夸谄媚的辞令仅仅适用于谈情说爱。这不仅是在言论上如此，因为一直都有这样一个很有见地的说法，说人主要吹嘘的是自己，但情人要算例外。情人眼里出西施，再自大的人也都不会夸张至此。所以，有人很精辟地说过："人在爱情中不会聪明。"这种缺点并非只有旁观者可见，并非被爱的一方看不见——除非这种爱是相互的。

铁定的规律是，爱情所得到的回报，从来都是要么得到爱的回应，要么得到对方内心隐隐的轻蔑。因此，人们更应小心对待这种情欲，它不但使人失去其他的东西，连爱情自己也保不住。至于其他方面的损失，诗人的诗史刻画得极好，说那个喜欢海伦的人放弃了朱诺和帕拉斯的礼物。凡是沉迷于爱情的人就会丢弃财富和智慧。

both riches and wisdom.

This passion hath his floods, in very times of weakness; which are great prosperity, and great adversity; though this latter hath been less observed. Both which times kindle love, and make it more fervent, and therefore show it to be the child of folly.

They do best, who if they cannot but admit love, yet make it keep quarters; and sever it wholly from their serious affairs, and actions, of life; for if it checks once with business, it troubleth men's fortunes, and maketh men, that they can no ways be true to their own ends. I know not how, but martial men are given to love: I think, it is but as they are given to wine; for perils commonly ask to be paid in pleasures.

There is in man's nature, a secret inclination and motion, towards love of others, which if it be not spent upon some one or a few, doth naturally spread itself towards many, and maketh the man become humane and charitable; as it is seen sometime in friars.

Nuptial love maketh mankind; friendly love perfecteth it; but wanton love corrupteth, and embaseth it.

每当人处于脆弱状态时，即最亨通和最受挫时，这种情欲就泛滥成灾，虽然人在最受挫时也有此问题一直是较少人注意的。这两种状态都在引燃爱火并使其热烈，因此可见，爱情是愚昧之子。

有些人处理得极好，当他们非爱不可的时候，就予以节制，并使之与其重大任务和人生主旨彻底分离，因为爱情一旦掺和到正事上，就会破坏人的运气，使人再也无法持守自己既定的目标。我不明白，为什么武士们都是耽于爱情的，我想这和他们好酒是一样的吧，因为冒险多是需要快感作报酬的。

人性中有一种深藏的主动爱人的倾向和动机，若无具体对象得以倾注，它便会撒向大众，并使人变得仁厚而慈善，正如有时在天主教修道士身上所见到的情形。

夫妻的爱，使人类繁衍；朋友的爱，给人以帮助；荒淫纵欲的爱，却只会使人堕落。

单词解析 Word Analysis

siren ['saɪrən] *n.* 汽笛；妖冶而危险的女人；危险的诱惑；塞壬（古希腊传说中半人半鸟的女海妖，惯以美妙的歌声引诱水手，使他们的船只或触礁或驶入危险水域）

例 It sounds like an air raid siren.
那听起来像是空袭警报。

fury ['fjʊri] *n.* 狂怒；暴怒；[罗神]复仇三女神之一；激怒者

例 She screamed, her face distorted with fury and pain.
她尖叫着，脸部因狂怒和痛苦而扭曲。

whereof [weər'ʌv] *adv.* （疑问副词）关于什么，（关系副词）关于那事（人，物），以什么的

例 Neither can they prove the things whereof they now accuse me.
他们现在所告我的事并不能向你证实了。

hath [hæθ] <废> have的第三人称单数现在式 = has

例 This man hath my consent to marry her.
这个人得到了我的允许和她结婚。

fortified ['fɔːtəfaɪd] *adj.* 加强的 *v.* 筑防御工事于（fortify的过去式和过去分词）；筑堡于；增强；强化（食品）

例 It has also been fortified with vitamin C.
它还添加了维生素C。

magnum ['mægnəm] *n.* 大酒瓶（容量约为2/5加仑）

例 This magnum opus took ten years to complete.
这部巨著历时十年始告成。

contemplation [ˌkɑːntəm'pleɪʃn] *n.* 沉思；凝视；注视；意图

例 He was lost in the contemplation of the landscape.
他对着眼前的景色沉思起来。

absurdly [əb'sɜːdlɪ] *adv.* 荒谬地，荒唐地

例 You are so absurdly bashful.
你腼腆的那么可笑。

doth [dʌθ] ⓥ do的第三人称单数现在式 = does

例 But my people have changed their glory for that which doth not profit.

但我的百姓将他们的荣耀换了那无益的神。

reciprocal [rɪˈsɪprəkəl] *adj.* 互惠的；倒数的；相互的 *n.* 倒数；互相关联的事物

例 They expected a reciprocal gesture before more hostages could be freed.

在更多人质获得自由之前他们期望看到对方也有相应的表示。

语法知识点 *Grammar Points*

① **For as to the stage, love is ever matter of comedies, and now and then of tragedies; but in life it does much mischief; sometimes like a siren, sometimes like a fury.**

这个句子中有一个结构"now and then"，表示"间或，有时候"。相当于 sometimes、from time to time 和 occasionally 等。

例 This section of the road is so narrow that there are bound to be traffic jams now and then.

这段路太窄，交通有时不免堵塞。

② **...and therefore it seems though rarely that love can find entrance, not only into an open heart, but also into a heart well fortified, if watch be not well kept.**

这个句子中有一个结构"not only...but also..."，表示"不仅……而且……"。

例 Not only I but also she is enjoying the film.

不仅是我，她也很喜欢这部电影。

③ **That it is impossible to love, and to be wise.**

这个句子中有一个结构"it is impossible to do"，表示"做某事不可能"。一般it is+形容词+for sb to do sth. 表示"对于某人来说，做某事很……"。

例 It is impossible to root out this disease in a few years.

要想在几年内根除这种疾病是不可能的。

④ **By how much the more, men ought to beware of this passion, which lose not only other things, but itself!**

这个句子中有两个结构"ought to do"和"beware of"，分别表示"应该做某事"和"小心，谨防"。前者相当于should。

例 You ought to examine yourself honestly and find out the source of your erroneous views.

你应该老老实实地反躬自省，找出你这些错误观点的根源。

Visitors should beware of pickpockets who often work in teams.

游客要小心那里团体作案的小偷。

经典名句 *Famous Classics*

1. To love a woman, usually the way she is; to love a young boy, and usually look at his future.

爱慕一个女子，通常爱她现在的样子；爱慕一个少年，通常着眼于他未来的样子。

2. Spring without flowers and life without love cannot form a world.

春天没有花，人生没有爱，那还成个什么世界。

3. Moderate love lasts long.

适度的爱情才会维持久远。

4. Love each other, but don't make love bond.

彼此互爱，但不要被爱束缚。

5. The one who says I do not love, is in love.

谁口口声声说我不爱，谁就在爱。

读书笔记

24 Call with Love
让爱相随

Unconsciously	在不知不觉间
We had already **mutually** known and loved each other for so many days	我们已经相知相恋了这么多的日子
You are always running away	你总是在回避
And I am always running after	而我却在不断地追寻
Whatever voice it is	不管是哪一个声音
We all can	我们都可以
wholeheartedly listen to it	用心倾听
Probably	或许
Among a sea of people	在茫茫人海里
We can't go forward hand in hand	我们不能携手前行
I still want to **make great efforts**	我还是要努力
To let you stay at the **bottom** of my heart	努力地让你的气息留在我的心底
And not to let missing you become a kind of **disease**	不要让思念成为一种病

单词解析 *Word Analysis*

unconsciously [ʌnˈkɑːnʃəsli] *adv.* 失去知觉地，无意识地；无意地，不自觉地；不受意识控制地

例 By the time ambulance men arrived he was lying there unconsciously.
救护人员到达时，他已经不省人事了。

mutually [ˈmjuːtʃuəli] *adv.* 互相地，互助地

例 Their interests were mutually incompatible.
他们俩的利益相抵触。

make great efforts 努力

例 I will make great efforts more! I will bring you the color!
我会更加努力！我会带给你们色彩！

bottom ['bɑːtəm] *n.* 底部；末端；臀部；尽头 *adj.* 底部的 *v.* 装底；测量深浅；查明真相；到达底部；建立基础

例 He sat at the bottom of the stairs.
他坐在最下面的一级楼梯上。

disease [dɪˈziːz] *n.* 疾病；弊端；不安 *v.* 传染；使……有病

例 Is this disease hereditary?
这种病遗传吗？

语法知识点 *Grammar Points*

① You are always running away/And I am always running after

这句话中有两个结构 "run away" 和 "run after"，分别表示 "逃跑" 和 "追赶"。后者一般加宾语，表示追赶某人或者某物，如run after him。

例 She started to run away and barged into a passer-by.
她拔腿逃跑，一下子和一位行人撞了个满怀。
David ran after the thief.
大卫追赶小偷。

② Among a sea of people/We can't go forward hand in hand.

这句话中有两个结构 "a sea of" 和 "hand in hand"，分别表示 "大量的，茫茫一片" 和 "手牵手"。

例 In reality, we belong to one galaxy in a sea of galaxies.
现实中，我们只是星系海洋中的一个星系。
But in days to come he will walk hand in hand with us.
但是在未来的日子里，他会跟我们携手同行。

③ I still want to make great efforts/To let you stay at the bottom of my heart

这句话中有三个结构 "make great efforts to do"， "let sb. do" 和 "at the bottom of"，分别表示 "努力干某事"， "让某人干某事" 和 "在……

的底部"。其中，let是使役动词，和make的用法一样。

例 China would make great efforts to kill poverty and achieve the MDGs in China on time.

中国将进一步加大扶贫开发力度，使千年发展目标在中国大地上如期实现。

Let them do it at once.

让他们马上做这件事。

They remain at the bottom of my closet, a shrine to her memory.

它们躺在衣柜的底层，那个属于她的回忆的神圣角落。

经典名句 *Famous Classics*

1. The water of the fountain does not die, and the fire of love does not die.

喷泉的水堵不死，爱情的火扑不灭。

2. Keep faith and silence for the people I love.

对我所爱的人保持信赖和沉默。

3. Love will find a way out.

爱情会自寻出路。

4. Genius only means hard-working in all one's life.

天才只意味着终身不懈地努力。

5. The man who has made up his mind to win will never say "impossible".

凡是决心取得胜利的人是从来不说"不可能的"。

读书笔记

25 Living a Life of Love
让生活充满爱

The key to living a life of love, peace and **prosperity** is to live from your heart.

When you live from your heart, you feel full and rich; and life seems to flow **effortlessly**. You feel in control, confident, and connected to your life's **purpose**. You feel joy and deep inner peace. You feel alive!

When love **radiates** from your heart you feel **vibrant**, energized and **blissful**. The feeling of being on purpose **inspires** you to new heights... some you never dreamed possible.

Living from your heart keeps you focused on what is most important to you in your life. You move from focusing on conflict to re-focusing on what is most important to you... Your deepest heart's desires.

In your heart holds the secret to true happiness. The secret is love. Love is the **tender** expression of the heart... an expression we all long to feel deep within.

Whether you know it or not, one of the most important relationships in your life is with your soul. Be kind and loving to your soul, and use all of your experiences as opportunities to **nourish** your soul!

让生活充满爱和安宁并且感觉富足的关键是真心实意地生活。

如果你真心实意地生活，就能感觉到心满意足，生活似乎总是称心如意的。你能掌握命运，充满自信，并且实现目标。你能感受到内心的喜悦与宁静。你会感到活力十足！

发自内心的爱让你觉得充满活力、精神焕发、幸福无比。这种感觉能激发你的灵感，向生活的新高度攀登……这是你以前从没想到过的。

真心实意地生活让你关注在你生命中最重要的东西。这样你的视线便逐渐远离纷争，转向对你而言更为重要的事情……你内心深处的渴望。

你的心中埋藏着幸福的秘密，那就是爱。爱是心灵温柔的表达，一种我们都渴望体会的深层感情的表达。

无论你知道与否，你生命中最重要的一种关系就是你与心灵的关系。关爱你的心灵，并把你所有的经历作为滋养心灵的一次次机会。

单词解析 *Word Analysis*

prosperity [prɑː'sperəti] *n.* 繁荣；成功；兴旺，昌盛

例 He was pursuing a utopian dream of world prosperity.
他怀揣着一个实现世界繁荣的乌托邦之梦。

effortlessly ['efətləslɪ] *adv.* 不做努力地，不费力地

例 There is so much information you can almost effortlessly find the facts for yourself.
资料这么多，你几乎可以毫不费力地找到事实真相。

purpose ['pɜːrpəs] *n.* 目的；意志；作用；（进行中的）行动 *v.* 有意；打算；企图（做）；决意（做）

例 For all practical purposes the treaty has already ceased to exist.
实际上协议已经不复存在。

radiate ['redi,et] *v.* 辐射；发射；使向周围扩展；发散；发光 *adj.* 辐射状的；射出的

例 Her voice hadn't changed but I felt the anger that radiated from her.
尽管她声音没变，但我还是感受到了她所流露出的怒气。

vibrant ['vaɪbrənt] *adj.* 振动的；响亮的；充满生气的

例 She possessed the vibrant personality that is so often popularly associated with Spanish women.
她拥有通常会令人联想到西班牙女性的火热个性。

blissful ['blɪsfl] *adj.* 极乐；极快乐的，极幸福的；充满喜悦的；有造化的

例 I had nine blissful hours of sleep.
我无忧无虑地酣睡了九个小时。

inspire [ɪn'spaɪə(r)] *v.* 激励；鼓舞；启迪；赋予灵感

例 Our challenge is to motivate those voters and inspire them to join our cause.
我们面临的挑战是如何调动那些选民的积极性并鼓励他们加入我们的事业。

tender ['tɛndə] *adj.* 温柔的；嫩的；纤弱的；疼痛的 *n.* 投标；（正式）提出；供应船，联络船；照看者

例 My tummy felt very tender.
我的肚子很疼。

nourish ['nɜːrɪʃ] *v.* 滋养，施肥于；抚养，教养；怀抱（希望、怨恨）；使健壮

例 A great variety of animals nourish themselves on vegetable foods.
绝大多数动物是食草的。

语法知识点 *Grammar Points*

① The key to living a life of love, peace and prosperity is to live from your heart.

这句话中有一个结构 "the key to sth./doing sth."，表示 "做某事的关键"。这里to是介词。

例 It is the key to everything.
它是通向一切的钥匙。

② You feel in control, confident, and connected to your life's purpose.

这句话中有一个结构 "in control" 和 "be connected to"，分别表示 "控制，管理" 和 "和……有联系"。后者相当于be related to。

例 You have to be lucid and in control.
你必须保持清醒和自控。

It is therefore connected to an end node.
因此它是连接到某个末端结点的。

③ You move from focusing on conflict to re-focusing on what is most important to you…

这个句子中有一个结构 "focus on"，表示 "集中精力于"。相当于concentrate on。

例 Close your eyes, and focus on your breathing.
闭上眼集中精力于你的呼吸。

经典名句 *Famous Classics*

1. Love keeps the cold out better than a cloak.
爱比大衣更能驱走寒冷。

2. My heart is with you.
我的心与你同在。

3. Wherever you go, whatever you do, I will be right here waiting for you.
无论你身在何处，无论你为何忙碌，我都会在此为你守候。

4. Passionate love is a quenchless thirst.
热烈的爱情是不可抑制的渴望。

5. The most precious possession that ever comes to a man in this world is a woman's heart.
在这个世界上，男人最珍贵的财产就是一个女人的心。

读书笔记

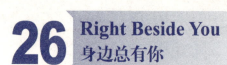

26 Right Beside You
身边总有你

The passengers on the bus watched **sympathetically** as the young woman with the white **cane** made her way carefully up the steps. She paid the driver and then, using her hands to feel the location of the seats, settled in to one. She placed her **briefcase** on her lap and rested her cane against her leg.

It had been a year since Susan, thirty-four, became blind. As the result of a medical accident she was **sightless**, suddenly thrown into a world of darkness, anger, **frustration** and self-pity. All she had to **cling** to was her husband Mark.

Mark was an Air Force officer and he loved Susan with all his heart. When she first lost her sight, he watched her sink into despair and he became determined to use every means possible to help his wife.

Finally, Susan felt ready to return to her job, but how would she get there? She used to take the bus, but she was now too frightened to get around the city by herself. Mark **volunteered** to ride the bus with Susan each morning and evening until she got the hang of it. And that is exactly what happened.

手持白手杖的年轻女子小心翼翼地上车时，车上的乘客都向她投去怜悯的目光。付了车费之后，女子双手摸索着座位坐好，然后把公文包放在膝盖上，手杖靠着腿。

三十四岁的苏珊一年前失明。一起医疗事故夺去了她的双眼，让她顿时陷入黑暗之中，内心充满愤怒、沮丧，还顾影自怜。而她唯一可以依靠的只有丈夫马克。

马克是名空军军官，他深爱着苏珊。苏珊失明的头些日子，他眼睁睁地看着妻子陷入绝望，心里打定主意，要尽一切办法帮助她。

苏珊终于愿意重返工作岗位了。可她怎么去上班呢？以前都是乘公交车去的，但她现在很害怕，不敢自己一个人在城里转。于是马克自告奋勇早晚坐公车接送苏珊，直到她可以一个人应付一切。这就是事情的经过。

整整两周，马克每天都穿着军装，陪着苏珊一起上下班，教她怎么凭借其他感官，尤其

For two weeks, Mark, in **military** uniform from head to feet, accompanied Susan to and from work each day. He taught her how to rely on her other senses, specifically her hearing, to determine where she was and how to adapt to her new environment. He helped her befriend the bus drivers who could watch out for her, and save her a seat.

Each morning they made the journey together, and Mark would take a taxi back to his office. Although that meant he had to travel through the city and the routine was costly and exhausting, Mark knew it was only a matter of time before Susan would be able to ride the bus on her own. He believed in her.

Finally, Susan decided that she was ready to try the trip on her own. Monday morning arrived. Before she left, she embraced her husband tightly. Her eyes filled with tears of gratitude for his loyalty, his patience, and his love. She said goodbye and, for the first time, they went their separate ways. Monday, Tuesday, Wednesday, Thursday… Each day on her own went perfectly, and a wild **gaiety** took hold of Susan. She was doing it! She was going to work all by herself!

On Friday morning, Susan took the bus to work as usual. As she was exiting the bus, the driver said, "Miss, I sure

是听觉，判断她所处的位置，以及如何适应新的环境。他还和司机说好了，这样司机就能照顾她，并给她留个座位。

每天早上，他们都一起出门，然后马克再乘出租车回去上班。尽管马克需要穿过整座城市，既劳累又费钱，但他坚信苏珊一定可以独立乘车，一切只是时间问题。

最后，苏珊决定自己独自坐车上班。星期一上午，临行前，她紧紧地拥抱了自己的丈夫，感激的泪水在眼眶打转，感谢他的忠诚，他的耐心，还有他的爱。她向他道了别，俩人第一次朝着不同的方向走去。周一、周二、周三、周四……每天她的独行之旅都很顺利，苏珊感到一阵狂喜。她成功了！她真的可以一个人去上班了！

周五早上，苏珊照常乘公共汽车去上班。就要下车了，司机说："小姐，我真羡慕你啊。"苏珊感到很奇怪，便问司机为什么。

"是这样的，上星期，每天早上都有一个仪表堂堂穿着军装的男士一直站在拐弯处看着你下车，看着你安全地穿过街道，又看着你走进办公楼，他向你飞一个吻，冲你行个

envy you." Being curious, Susan asked the driver why.

"You know, every morning for the past week, a fine-looking gentleman in a military uniform has been standing across the corner watching you when you get off the bus. He makes sure you cross the street safely and he watches you until you enter your office building. Then he blows you a kiss, gives you a **salute** and walks away. You are one lucky lady." the bus driver said.

Tears of happiness poured down Susan's cheeks. She was so lucky for he had given her a gift more powerful than sight, a gift she didn't need to see to believe—the gift of love that can bring light where there is darkness.

礼，然后才转身离去。你真是个幸运的姑娘！"司机说。

苏珊流下幸福的泪水。她是幸运的，因为马克给了她比视力更珍贵的礼物，一份没有视力也能体会到的礼物——这就是爱的礼物，它能给黑暗带来光明。

单词解析 Word Analysis

sympathetically [ˌsɪmpəˈθetɪklɪ] *adv.* 悲怜地，富有同情心地

例 They would invite him back and listen sympathetically to his woes.
他们将邀请他回来并同情地倾听他的不幸遭遇。

cane [keɪn] *n.* 手杖；（植物的）茎；棍棒，棒；藤条，藤料

例 Bamboo produces an annual crop of cane.
竹子每年都能长出一批竹竿。

briefcase [ˈbrif,kes] *n.* 公文包；公事包；手提箱；手提包

例 I should not leave my briefcase and camera bag unguarded.
我不该把我的公文包和相机包留在那儿无人看管。

sightless ['saɪtlɪs] *adj.* 无视力的，盲的

例 He wiped a tear from his sightless eyes.
他从瞎了的眼睛里擦去了一滴泪水。

frustration [frʌ'streʃən] *n.* 挫折；挫败；失意；失败

例 Frustration, anger and desperation have led to a series of wildcat strikes.
挫败感、愤怒和绝望引起了一系列自发性的罢工。

cling [klɪŋ] *v.* 坚持；附着于，紧贴；抓紧或抱住；沿（岸）前进，贴着（墙）走；依恋

例 Another man was rescued as he clung to the riverbank.
另外一个人因为紧紧攀住河堤而获救。

volunteer [,vɑ:lən'tɪr] *n.* 志愿者，志愿兵 *adj.* 自愿的，志愿的 *v.* 自愿去做；当志愿兵

例 She now helps in a local school as a volunteer three days a week.
目前她在当地的一家学校做志愿者工作，一周去3天。

military ['mɪləteri] *adj.* 军事的；军用的；讨厌的；好战的 *n.* 军队；军人；武装力量

例 Military action may become necessary.
也许有必要采取军事行动。

gaiety ['geɪəti] *n.* 快乐；高兴；作乐；花哨

例 Music rang out adding to the gaiety and life of the market.
音乐响起来了，给市场增添了一份快乐和生机。

salute [sə'lut] *v.* 欢迎，致敬；向……致意；赞扬，赞颂 *n.* 敬礼；致敬，欢迎；举枪，举刀（礼）

例 One of the company stepped out and saluted the General.
人群中走出一人向将军敬礼。

语法知识点 *Grammar Points*

① **The passengers on the bus watched sympathetically as the young woman with the white cane made her way carefully up the steps.**

这个句子中有一个结构"make one's way"，表示"前往"。

 And as soon as I've got the eggs for you, I'll make my way home along the tree-tops.

替你们取到蛋后，我就要沿着树顶走回家的。

② **As the result of a medical accident she was sightless, suddenly thrown into a world of darkness, anger, frustration and self-pity.**

这个句子中有一个结构"as the result of"，表示"由于……的原因"。相当于 because of 和 due to。

 The Seattle Times apologized for the mistake, describing it as the result of sloppy editing.

《西雅图时报》为这一错误标题道了歉，说这是编辑掉以轻心的结果。

③ **When she first lost her sight, he watched her sink into despair and he became determined to use every means possible to help his wife.**

这句话中有三个结构"sink into"、"become determined to do"和"use every means to do"，分别表示"陷入，沉入"、"下决心做某事"和"用尽方法做某事"。

 You cannot sink into quicksand.

你不会陷入流沙。

Had you determined to become a graduate student?

你决定要读研究生了吗？

They will use every means at their disposal to distract you from your path.

他们将运用一切手段让你偏离自己的道路。

④ **He taught her how to rely on her other senses, specifically her hearing, to determine where she was and how to adapt to her new environment.**

这句话中有两个结构"rely on"和"adapt to"，分别表示"依赖"和"适应"。前者同义词组还有 depend on，on 可以换成 upon。

Our defences rely on what we can plan and do now.
我们的防线依赖于我们现在能计划和执行的措施。

We should adapt to it.
我们必须适应它。

⑤ **Each day on her own went perfectly, and a wild gaiety took hold of Susan.**

这句话中有一个结构"take hold of"，表示"吸引住，抓住"。相当于 catch 和 grab。

 How must I take hold of you in order not to hurt you?
我应当怎样抱，才不会弄痛您呢？

经典名句 *Famous Classics*

1. Love is like a war, easy to begin but hard to end.
爱就像一场战争，开战容易停火难。

2. Love opens your chest and opens your heart and it means someone can get inside you and mess you up.
爱扒开你的胸膛，掏出你的心脏，让人乘机侵入你的内心把你搞得一团糟。

3. Does God punish or reward us with love?
爱，是上帝用来惩罚我们的还是奖赏我们的呢？

4. Love your neighbor, but don't get caught.
爱你的邻家女孩吧，但注意不要无法自拔。

5. The way to love anything is to realize that it might be lost.
珍爱一切的好办法是：意识到你可能会失去它。

27 Tommy and Sabrina
汤米和塞布丽娜

Tommy was eleven and Sabrina soon would be.

Every morning they would meet beside the big **oak tree**.

In the summer, they would play together in the sun.

And sit **beneath** the big oak tree when the day was done.

One time when they were talking of growing up some day.

They agreed they'd meet back there and maybe even stay.

By the big oak tree they could build a little home.

And they would be together and neither one would **roam**.

When Tommy was thirteen and Sabrina soon would be.

They stood together one last time beside the big oak tree.

Tommy had to leave for his family soon would move.

He took his **pocketknife** and in the big oak made a **groove**.

The groove was Tommy's simple way of giving her his word.

As he spoke so **softly**, this was what Sabrina heard:

"On your eighteenth birthday, I'll

汤米十一岁，塞布丽娜也要满十一岁了。

每天清晨，他们就在那棵大橡树下见面。

夏天，他们在阳光下一起打闹。

到了晚上，就坐在大橡树下休息。

一次，他们正谈论着他们长大的那天。

他们约定会再回到这里，甚至就此留下。

他们在大橡树旁建一个小屋。

彼此不离不弃，谁也不离开谁。

汤米十三岁了，塞布丽娜也要十三岁了。

他们最后一次一起站在大橡树旁。

汤米很快就要离开家，搬去其他地方。

他取出随身小刀，在大橡树上刻了一道痕。

这道痕是汤米对她真挚的承诺。

随后，汤米轻轻地对塞布丽娜说：

"在你十八岁生日时，我

return to our oak tree.

Then we will be together forever-you and me."

City life was **hectic** and the years did quickly fly.

Tommy never once forgot Sabrina's last good-bye.

He had marked the **calendar** each year on her birthday.

Soon he'd see the big oak tree and, maybe, even stay.

He would hold Sabrina's hand; together they'd agree.

To stay beside each other—close to the big oak tree.

Tommy **headed for** the tree one Sunday afternoon.

It was her eighteenth birthday and he would see her soon.

When Tommy reached the tree, he found a written note.

It was from Sabrina's mom, and here was what she wrote:

"Sabrina cannot meet you; she won't be here today.

In this **envelope** is what Sabrina has to say."

He opened up the letter and his hands began to **shake**.

As he read Sabrina's words, his heart began to break.

"Tommy, dear, I know that you are standing by our tree.

会回到我们的大橡树下，

然后我们永远地在一起——只有你和我。"

城市生活十分繁忙，几年匆匆而过。

汤米从来没有忘记塞布丽娜的最后一次告别。

每年都会在日历上标记出她的生日。

不久，他就会再次见到那棵大橡树，也许，甚至就待在那里了。

他会握着塞布丽娜的手，如约定一般在一起。

彼此守护——紧紧地依靠在大橡树旁。

一个星期天下午，汤米前往大橡树。

这是她十八岁的生日，他马上就可以见到她了。

汤米到那棵树下时，发现一张纸条。

那是塞布丽娜的妈妈留下的，她写道：

"塞布丽娜不能和你见面了，她今天也不会来了。

这封信里有塞布丽娜想说的。"

他打开信封，手在颤抖。

他读着信，心都碎了。

"汤米，亲爱的，我知道你此时此刻正站在我们的树旁。

当你看到我们的大橡树

When you see the big oak tree, you always think of me.

"I won't be here to meet you; the Angels came my way.

Nothing else would keep me from meeting you today.

Look up in the sky, and you'll know that I can see,

You standing there and waiting-beside our big oak tree."

时，你想的都是我。

我不能来这里见你了；天使已经带去了我的思念。

没有什么能阻挡我来见你。

抬头望望天空，你会知道我可以看见你。

看见你站在我们的大橡树旁等待着。"

单词解析 *Word Analysis*

oak tree [əʊktriː] *n.* 橡树；柞树

例 An oak tree cast its shadow over a tiny round pool.
一棵橡树的影子投射在一洼圆形的小水池上。

beneath [bɪ'niːθ] *prep.* 在……的下方；（表示等级）低于；（表示状态）在……掩饰之下；（表示环境）在……影响之下 *adv.* 在下面；在底下

例 Somewhere deep beneath the surface lay a caring character.
在内心深处的某个角落里埋藏着一颗爱心。

pocketknife ['pɑːkɪtnaɪf] *n.* 随身小折刀

例 Steven killed the bird with his pocketknife.
史蒂文用随身带的小刀杀死了这只小鸟。

groove [gruv] *n.* 沟，槽；（车）辙；节奏

例 The groove is too deep.
这个槽挖得太深了。

roam [roʊm] *v.* 漫游；漫步 *n.* 漫步，漫游

例 Barefoot children roamed the streets.
光脚丫的孩子们在街上游荡。

softly ['sɔːftli] *adv.* 柔和地；柔软地；静静地；温和地

例 She knelt and brushed her lips softly across Michael's cheek.
她跪了下来，轻吻迈克尔的脸颊。

hectic ['hɛktɪk] *adj.* 繁忙的，忙乱的；兴奋的，狂热的；（因患肺病等）发烧的；患热病的 *n.* 肺病热患者；[医]潮红

例 You have had a hectic day.
你们辛苦了一整天。

calendar ['kæləndə] *n.* 日历；历法；日程表；（一年之中的）重大事件（或重要日期）一览表

例 They tried to make a calendar of Spain's festivals.
他们打算做个西班牙节日活动一览表。

head for 走向；朝……进发；<非正> 引向好（坏）结果；奔

例 In the winter I head for the mall.
在冬日里，我前往这个购物商场。

envelope ['envələup] *n.* 信封，封皮；壳层，外壳；包裹物；[生物学] 膜，包袋

例 He gave me the envelope and we parted.
他给了我那个信封，我们就告别了。

shake [ʃek] *v.* 动摇；摇头；使发抖；使心绪不宁；握手抖（掉）；（嗓音）颤抖 *n.* 震动；摇动；哆嗦；混合饮料

例 As soon as he got inside, the dog shook himself.
他一进来，狗就开始摇头摆尾。

语法知识点 *Grammar Points*

① One time when they were talking of growing up some day.

这个句子中有两个结构 "talk of" 和 "grow up"，分别表示"谈起"和"长大"。前者相当于 talk about。

例 In the coffee house, they talk of the new mathematics for calculating probability.

坐在咖啡馆里的人们在谈论着新的用来计算概率的数学。

This is where you have to grow up.

这就是你要成长的地方。

② Tommy had to leave for his family soon would move.

这个句子中有两个结构"have to"和"leave for"，分别表示"不得不，必须"和"动身去"。前者同义词还有must，must表示主观不得不，have to表示客观方面；后者相当于go to和head for。

例 They have to vacate their offices before Wednesday.

他们必须在星期三前将办公室腾出来。

He asked me yesterday when I should leave for Paris.

昨天他问我什么时候动身去巴黎。

经典名句 *Famous Classics*

1. Pain past is pleasure.

过去的痛苦就是快乐。

2. While there is life, there is hope.

留得青山在，不怕没柴烧。

3. Wisdom in the mind is better than money in the hand.

脑中有知识，胜过手中有金钱。

4. Storms make trees take deeper roots.

风暴使树木深深扎根。

5. Nothing is impossible for a willing heart.

心之所愿，无所不成。

28 Though Single, I Am Happy A
我单身，我快乐A

I was satisfied when I was first engaged with this "big name" company which has once designed the tallest building in China. I've since realized that this is just another "No Life" company living on its name. So, in fact I still don't have a life and I've discovered that I am screwed and **destined** to contribute my soul for a sound job title and reasonable salary.

I think about work from the moment I wake. Aesthesia sets in every morning with birdcall and I follow my senses and the ritual of trying to use the least amount of time to deal with trivial but **essential** routines; choosing the "best" food that is easiest to be swallowed and digested; reducing water ingestion to avoid unnecessary wastage and thus wasted time **scurrying off** for toilet visits; forever perfecting shortened "bye-byes" to get out the door more rapidly; enhancing work productivity after waking by bringing remaining unfinished work that can be accessed between **naps**.

Thus every second saved gives an **extra** second to increased efficiency and output. As for any form of **unstructured** time, like seeing movies,

在我顺利加入这家曾设计过中国最高建筑的知名企业之初，我满意极了。然而，当我发觉这也不过是一家靠着名气吃饭的"无生活"公司时，满足感顿时消失。所以，实际上我还是过着"无生活"的生活，每天为了我响亮的头衔和合理的薪水全力打拼。

从睁开眼睛的那一刻开始，我满脑子就都是工作的事情；每天清晨被鸟叫声唤醒，凭着直觉用最短的时间处理掉吃喝拉撒之类生活必需的琐事；吃最容易咀嚼吞咽消化的食物；尽量少喝水，以减少频繁往返卫生间所侵占的时间；永远完美而简短地说再见并快速出门；尽量把一些当天没能处理完的事情留在睡梦中继续思考，以提高醒来后的工作效率……

就这样，从日常生活中挤出来的一分一秒让我有更充足的时间提高效率和超额完成工作量。至于什么休闲活动，譬如看电影、逛街，甚至只是干坐着发发呆，绝对是没门儿的，除非驱使我工作的"魔

strolling around, or even just being in a thoughtless **daze**, only when the devil is blind to work, time, efficiency and productivity will that time come for me.

I have turned so panda eyed, so much so that even liberal coverings of foundation make up can't conceal my physical signs of **exhaustion**. I am especially **numb** about my gender, as I was **disillusioned** with my MD's genuinely appreciative praise on my "manly" working attitude, which runs counter to my lifetime pursuit of becoming a full time **blissfully** happy housewife. But every time my real ambition becomes lost as I become, against my will, deeply emotionally connected with the MD by his impassioned speeches that are always full of his acknowledgement to those who work slave-like with bended heads over heaped papers. I hang on his words waiting for **tidbits** of praise and after I am filled with **self-loathing** that I am **sucked into** this **subordinate** and **subservient** role. And as a female I feel we have lost our gender and identity in the battlefield of the inner office, becoming sexless, senseless, and loveless, living our "No Life" existence.

Some people, it seems, do have a **constructive** consciousness and attitude towards working, always looking forward

鬼"已经完全瞎掉，看不到工作、时间、效率和业绩！

我脸上挂着两个黑黑的熊猫眼，它们是如此醒目地昭示着我的疲倦，以至于再浓的妆也掩盖不住。拼命的工作让我对自己的性别概念完全模糊，直到老板诚挚地夸奖我"男人般"的工作态度时，我才想起当年我对人生的美好设想是做一个幸福快乐的家庭主妇。可是，当我的老板激情洋溢地盛赞那些藏身于厚厚的文件背后、垂着脑袋像奴隶一般工作的员工时，我曾经的人生理想再一次完全隐匿。我渴望得到认同和表扬，而随后我又陷入极度的自我厌恶中，我竟然沉迷于这个卑微的奴性角色中。作为一名女性，我们在办公室没有硝烟的战场上渐渐丧失了自己的女性身份，变成一个个没有性别特征、没有意识、也没有爱情的"无生活"生物。

似乎有那么一种人，总是对工作有着建设性的觉悟和态度，每天都积极乐观地向前看，从不会消极怠工。曾经在电视上看到过一次对某位CEO的采访，他自豪地总结企业成功的秘诀："我们的成功，都归功于我们的员工披星戴月、夜以继日、积极快乐地工

and thinking positively, without **cynicism**. There was an interview with some CEO on TV **insolently summing-up** the secrets of success: "Our success is due to those personnel happily working for the enterprise day and night, day after day." I don't know whether these employees are really happy or **pretend** to be happy or if the CEO has assumed subjectively his staffs' happiness. I ask myself, can work really bring such contentment and fulfillment to my life?

作！"不知道他们是真的开心，还是看上去开心，抑或只是CEO们一厢情愿地主观假定他们应该很开心。我不禁自问，工作真的能给一个人带来那么大的满足感和成就感吗？

单词解析 *Word Analysis*

destine ['destɪn] *v.* 注定；预定；命定；指定

例 Some things destine that it is not yours.
有些东西注定不是你的。

essential [ɪ'sɛnʃəl] *adj.* 必要的；本质的；基本的；精华的 *n.* 必需品；基本要素；必不可少的东西

例 It was absolutely essential to separate crops from the areas that animals used as pasture.
将庄稼和放牧区分开绝对必要。

scurry off [法] 窜逃，匆忙逃开

例 They just needed to be monitored so they didn't scurry off in the wrong direction.
他们只需要稍加引导，以免误入歧途。

nap [næp] *n.* 绒毛；小睡，打盹；一种牌戏；孤注一掷 *v.* 打瞌睡；疏忽；使起毛

例 The security services were clearly caught napping.
保安工作明显有漏洞。

extra ['ekstrə] *adj.* 额外的，补充的，附加的；特大的，特别的 *n.* 附加物，额外的事物；临时演员

例 Police warned motorists to allow extra time to get to work.
警方告诫驾车者出门上班要留出富余时间。

unstructured [ʌn'strʌktʃərd] *adj.* 无社会组织的，未组织的

例 As seminars go, these are loose, unstructured affairs.
和多数研讨会一样，这些研讨会也比较松散随意。

daze [deiz] *v.* 使（某人）迷乱而不能做出正确反应，使茫然；使（某人）惊奇与迷惑

例 I left the ranch in a daze.
我茫然地离开了牧场。

exhaustion [ɪg'zɔstʃən] *n.* 疲惫，衰竭；枯竭，用尽；排空；彻底的研究

例 Staff said he is suffering from exhaustion.
员工说他极度疲劳。

numb [nʌm] *adj.* 麻木的，失去感觉的；无动于衷的，没感情的 *v.* 使麻木，使麻痹

例 He could feel his fingers growing numb at their tips.
他能感到指尖正在变得麻木。

disillusioned [ˌdɪsɪ'luːʒnd] *adj.* 幻想破灭的；大失所望的；醒悟的；不抱幻想的 *v.* 使不再抱幻想，使理想破灭（disillusion的过去式和过去分词）；唤醒

例 I've become very disillusioned with politics.
我对政治完全不再抱幻想了。

blissfully ['blɪsfəlɪ] *adv.* 幸福地，充满喜悦地

例 He spent his blissfully carefree childhood in the countryside.
他在乡下度过了他无忧无虑的幸福童年。

tidbit ['tɪd,bɪt] *n.* 趣闻；（美味食物的）一口；小片珍馐；小栏报道

例 The team is also fending off the ravenous English tabloids, hungering for whatever Beckham tidbit they can find.

球队还在努力挡开那些贪婪的英国小报，他们饥渴地想要找到任何和贝克汉姆有关的珍闻。

self-loathing ['selfl'oʊðɪŋ] *n.* 自我讨厌的；自我憎恨的

例 After years of bullying and self-loathing, Taylor found her confidence when she joined a modelling agency.
经历了多年的欺凌和自我憎恨，泰勒在加入了一个模特社团之后找到了自信。

suck into <英俚> 拍……马屁，巴结

例 I'm serious, they'll try and suck you into their elderly ways.
我是说真的，他们会把你变成老人。

subordinate [sə'bɔːrdɪnət] *adj.* 下级的；级别或职位较低的；次要的；附属的 *n.* 部属；部下，下级 *v.* 使……居下位，使在次级；使服从；使从属

例 Haig tended not to seek guidance from subordinates.
黑格不愿向下属请教。

subservient [səb'sɜːrviənt] *adj.* 卑躬屈节的；有帮助的；充当下手的；马屁精

例 She is expected to be subservient to her uncle.
她被要求对叔叔恭敬顺从。

constructive [kən'strʌktɪv] *adj.* 建设的，建设性的；积极的，有助益的；构造上的

例 She welcomes constructive criticism.
她欢迎建设性的批评。

cynicism ['sɪnɪˌsɪzəm] *n.* 玩世不恭；愤世嫉俗；讥笑，讥讽的言辞；犬儒哲学，犬儒主义

例 I found Ben's cynicism wearing at times.
我有时觉得本的愤世嫉俗令人厌烦。

insolently ['ɪnsələntlɪ] *adv.* 自豪地，自傲地

例 Julia turns her head, and stares insolently at Charteris.
朱丽叶转过头来，傲慢地瞪着查特里斯。

summing-up ['sʌmɪŋ'ʌp] *n.* 总结

（例） Finally, this paper makes a summing-up for encountered problems in research, and proposals reasonable ameliorated orientation.

最后本论文对研究中遇到的问题进行了总结，并提出合理的改进方向。

pretend [prɪ'tend] *v.* 伪装；假装；（尤指儿童在游戏中）装扮；自诩

（例） The captain was astern, pretending he was sleeping.

船长在船尾，假装睡着了。

contentment [kən'tɛntmənt] *n.* 满足，满意，知足，心满意足

（例） I cannot describe the feeling of contentment that was with me at that time.

我无法描述当时我满足的感觉。

语法知识点 *Grammar Points*

① **I was satisfied when I was first engaged with this "big name" company which has once designed the tallest building in China.**

这个句子中有一个结构"be engaged with"，表示"忙碌于，从事"。其中，the tallest表示最高级，形容词最高级前面加定冠词the。

（例） At present I'm engaged with the revision of my dictionary.

目前我正忙于修订我那部词典。

② **I've since realized that this is just another "No Life" company living on its name.**

这个句子中有一个结构"live on"，表示"以……为生，以……为食"。

（例） She loves the land and the people who live on it.

她热爱这片土地和生活在这片土地上的人们。

③ **Aesthesia sets in every morning with birdcall and I follow my senses and the ritual of trying to use the least amount of time to deal with trivial but essential routines…**

这个句子中有一个结构"deal with"，表示"处理，解决"。

（例） I can't deal with your personal problems.

我不能处理你的个人问题。

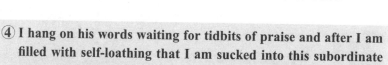
④ **I hang on his words waiting for tidbits of praise and after I am filled with self-loathing that I am sucked into this subordinate and subservient role.**

这个句子中有两个结构"be filled with"和"be sucked into"，分别表示"被……充满"和"吸入"。前者相当于be full of。

例 We were filled with hope, with passion, with dreams for the future.
我们浑身上下都是希望和激情，对未来充满了梦想。

Essentially, a black hole is a place where gravitational forces are so extreme that everything is sucked into it—including light.
本质上，黑洞是一个引力极大的物体，以至于任何物体，包括光，都会被它吸入。

经典名句 *Famous Classics*

1. Precious things are very few in this world. That is the reason there is just one you.
在这世上珍贵的东西总是罕有，所以这世上只有一个你。

2. You make my heart smile.
我的心因你而微笑。

3. Why do the good girls, always want the bad boys?
为何好女孩总喜欢坏男孩？

4. Being with you is like walking on a very clear morning.
和你在一起就像在一个清爽的早晨漫步。

5. Difficult circumstances serve as a textbook of life for people.
困难坎坷是人们的生活教科书。

29 Though Single, I Am Happy B
我单身，我快乐 B

I still remember in a meeting that our MD said that the previous manager here, who was female, quit the company because she could not get married and couldn't even get into any stable relationship due to the time she must give to her work! She was close to 50 before she realized the necessity to change jobs and priorities. Nearly 50 for Christ's sake! I promised myself I will never become the second sedulous example in this company. There is also a fashion designer who hasn't been in a relationship for 5 years. The last time she was in love was in university. She has No Life. She doesn't even have time for meals. She has resolved to break up with this company. How many are there like us? How many "No Life" women are there? There are two groups of women in Shanghai, and maybe in this world, 90% have "No Life", no fun and no money. The other 10% seems to make money easily, they go clubbing all week, drinking and partying, it seems this is their "Life". Because I am single, I am not a socialite, and I am deemed an older woman (approaching 30), am I destined to always work hard with "No

我仍然记得在一次会议上我老板提到的公司前任女经理的事情。据说她把所有时间都花在了工作上，以至于没空考虑结婚的事，甚至无法和一个男人维持稳定的关系，最后她只好辞掉工作。当她意识到必须要改变工作和生活的先后关系时，她已经年届五十了。五十岁啊，老天！我对自己发誓，我决不能成为第二个她！还有另一位时尚女设计师，已经整整五年没谈过恋爱了。她的上一次恋爱还得追溯到大学时代……她完全过着"无生活"的生活，甚至连吃饭的时间都没有。后来她终于下定决心离开了这家公司。还有多少人和我们有同样的经历？这里还有多少过着"无生活"的女性？在上海，甚至是全世界，女人只分为两种：90%"无生活"，没有情趣也没有钱；另外10%早早地赚够了钱，于是天天泡吧喝酒办派对，享受着看似精彩的"生活"。而我，因为还是单身，又不是什么社交名媛，又被归为大龄女性（年届三十），我就得乖乖地奴隶般地工作，过我的"无生活"

Life"?

I am a single older woman.

Sometimes I am a lonely woman.

I ask myself is that true? Am I old, single and lonely?

There are far too many **compatriots** in the same boat with me. What else can I say to you to convince you otherwise? Sometimes I can not even **convince** myself that I'm a success in someway—we are lonely, we long for love, we are terribly afraid of dying **destitute**. When Bella DePaulo, Ph.D., a **psychology** professor at the University of California, Santa Barbara, and author of the book *Singled Out* (St. Martin's Press, 2006), asked 950 college students to describe married people, they used words like "happy, loving, secure, stable, and kind." The **descriptions** of singles, on the other hand, included "lonely, shy, unhappy, insecure, inflexible, and **stubborn**". My goodness, am I one of them? I **screamed** and could not help asking myself this question. Mind you, nearly more then 50% of my friends who are far beyond their nubile age are still unmarried. There are several reasons for this: career women marry later; the divorce rate is high for many reasons, including pressure of work; little time and mood to share your darling's romance; no emotion to

生活吗？

我是个单身的大龄女性。

我时不时也会觉得寂寞。

是这样吗，我问自己？我真的又老又孤独吗？

无数女同胞和我在同一条船上。我还能说些什么呢？说什么才能让你相信事实并非如此呢？因为我们单身，渴望爱情，极端害怕孤独终老，所以有时候我甚至不能说服自己其实我在某些方面也算是获得了成功！在圣巴巴拉的加州大学分校任职并且即将发行新书*Singled Out*的心理学教授贝拉·德保罗博士，让950名学子来描述已婚人士，学生们用了诸如"幸福"、"相爱"、"可靠"、"稳定"、"美好"这类的词汇。而他们对未婚人群的形容，则是"孤独"、"羞涩"、"不幸"、"惶恐"、"固执"或是"执拗"。我不禁惊呼并不自觉地不断问自己："老天，莫非我也是他们中的一员？"事实上，我半数以上的女性朋友都已经远远过了适婚年龄却还是孤身一人。造成这个局面的原因有很多：不少职业女性打定主意要晚婚，因为工作压力等原因离婚率居高不下；心情很糟糕，根本没有心思去缓解另一半的压力，因为自己的压力都无处

release pressure from your hubby as you may also be stressed; no time or idea how to make proper **candlelit** dinners and, wow, just too many to list here. By the way, not to put too fine a point on it, those women who are married are likely to **outlive** their mates. As a result, most career women are now likely to spend more years of their lives **single** than with a significant other.

We singles are not birds of a feather. Is today's typical older **unwed** female a lot like Carrie Bradshaw, Sex and the City's free-spirited **patron saint** of the **deliberately** single? The answer: a little of this and a little of that, and in some cases, all kinds of excuses you could figure out.

Whatever, it's clear that words like lonely, shy, and insecure no longer apply to all. Fully half the women in our times, including me, say we are happier than we've ever been, at least while working and especially at the time we see and feel our careers progressing. Are we sad now and then? Sure—aren't we all? Do we occasionally lose sleep worrying about the future? Yes, and with good reason: being a single older woman comes with its own economic challenges. But that doesn't stop the majority from believing that **midlife** offers an opportunity for growth, for

释放；没有时间也完全没想过去营造一次烛光晚餐……哎呀，简直数不胜数！同时，虽然这一点听起来会让人觉得很不舒服，但事实上就算结了婚，女人往往也还是比男人长寿。所以这样一来，大部分职业女性单身一人的日子可能会比拥有爱人的日子长得多。

我们这些单身女性的情况各异。难道今天的典型大龄未婚女性都是《欲望都市》里的凯莉那样拥有自由灵魂的独身主义者吗？当然不是，有时候，单身的理由真的是千奇百怪，你可能想都想不到。

无论如何，有一点是肯定的，那就是诸如"孤独""羞涩""不安"这样的词汇已经完全不再适用于单身女性了。当今社会，至少半数的女性都认为自己过得异乎寻常的幸福。至少在工作中，特别是在看到或感觉到自己事业上取得的成就时，我们会这么觉得。我们是否也会时不时地感伤呢？毋庸置疑——大家不都是这样吗？我们偶尔是否会因为担心自己的将来而失眠呢？答案也是肯定的，而且我们有很好的理由：成为一个大龄的单身女性势必会带来一系列经济上的问题。但是这些并不能阻止大多数女性朝着单身又大龄这

learning, and the chance to do the things we've always wanted to do. We even have the chance to do things outside of the confines, restraints and **shackles** of a relationship.

So now, let me and all of you think again, do we really have "No Life"? I have some benefits that many married housewives can't share. Also, are we, the single "No Lifers", have created cages or limitations for ourselves? If so, it's in our hands to set ourselves free, to give ourselves "A Life", and not be so controlled by the expectations of society, work, family and friends who **patronize** us into thinking and believing that we have "No Life".

Am I desperate to find a mate? Given the option, I wouldn't mind a committed relationship with a cuddly, caring partner—preferably someone with minimal emotional **baggage** and the kind of income to support a nice summer house.

I do not feel like dating at times, just simply because I am not interested in dating or being in a romantic relationship with bald guys unless I meet someone really interesting. It requires a philosophical balance between putting on a game face on Saturday night and not getting stressed if nothing develops.

Am I lonely? I confess, yes I am,

条路走。她们仍然相信人到中年才拥有成长、学习的好时机，并有机会让自己可以随心所欲，甚至还能冲破重重阻碍和桎梏去做那些从前不被允许做或者做不到的事情。

所以现在，让我们大家再一起来思考一下，我们过的真的是"无生活"的生活吗？我生活中的一些乐趣是很多家庭妇女无法品尝到的。那么，我们这些单身的"无生活者"们又是不是在作茧自缚呢？如果是这样，我们应该亲手解放自己，自己给自己"生活者"，而不是让自己的思维被那些迫使我们相信自己是"无生活者"的社会、工作、家人和朋友所限制。

我真是那么迫切地要找到另一半吗？当然，如果可以选择的话，我倒是不介意去忠实于一个可爱又体贴的伴侣——当然他最好是没有过去的感情包袱，又有不少收入，最好可以附带买得起一套漂亮的房子。

可有时候我也没那么想去约会。原因很简单，除非那个男人真的很有趣，否则要去和一个秃顶的男人约会或者谈恋爱可真算不上是一件有意思的事！要想在周末晚上约会时显得轻松自在，又不能表现出因为担心两人关系没有进展而忧

but everyone is lonely sometimes—even married people. But I actually enjoy my solitude while it could more or less balance my stressful feeling. Living alone can be lonely for sure but I love the freedom, and the fact that I know so many other singles I can network with.

Do I like my manliness? Of course I don't. But I realized to have manliness in working is one thing and having it outside of work is another story completely. I am keenly aware that appearances matter in our society and as women we need to know when to be manly and when to be feminine.

心忡忡，如果没有一点哲学平衡思想是很难做到的。

我真的孤独吗？好吧，我承认，我是很孤独，但是人人都有孤独的时候，结没结婚都一样！但是孤独感有时候或多或少能平衡压力，这让我有时候也觉得孤独是一种享受。一个人生活当然会孤独，但我钟爱那种自由。事实上在我的周围有很多和我同样单身的人，我们都享受和彼此交流的乐趣。

我喜欢男人味吗？当然不是。但我清楚地知道，在工作中拥有男人味是一件拿得出手的事情，如果在工作中没有男人气概，那就是另一种结局了。我敏锐地意识到，呈现在当今社会的一个事实是，我们女人需要明白，什么时候该呈现女人味，什么时候该呈现男人味。

单词解析 *Word Analysis*

compatriot [kəmˈpeɪtrɪət] *n.* 同胞；同国人 *adj.* 同胞的；同国人的

例 Chris Robertson of Australia beat his compatriot Chris Dittmar in the final.
澳大利亚的克里斯·罗伯逊在决赛中击败了自己的同胞克里斯·迪特马。

convince [kənˈvɪns] *v.* 使相信，说服，使承认；使明白

例 Although I soon convinced him of my innocence, I think he still has serious doubts about my sanity.
虽然我很快便让他相信我是清白的，但是我想他仍然非常怀疑我是否神志正常。

destitute ['destɪtuːt] *adj.* 穷困的；极度缺乏的；贫乏的；无的 *n.* 赤贫者 *v.* 使穷困，使贫穷；夺去，使丧失

例 Many had lost all in the disaster and were destitute.
很多人被灾难夺去了一切，变得一无所有。

psychology [saɪˈkɑːlədʒi] *n.* 心理学；心理状态；心理特点；心理影响

例 He studied philosophy and psychology at Cambridge.
他在剑桥大学学习哲学和心理学。

description [dɪˈskrɪpʃən] *n.* 描述；形容；种类；类型

例 Events of this description occurred daily.
这类事件天天发生。

stubborn ['stʌbərn] *adj.* 顽固的，固执的；坚持的；棘手的

例 He is a stubborn character used to getting his own way.
他性格固执，惯于一意孤行。

scream [skriːm] *v.* 尖声喊叫，拼命叫喊；尖叫 *n.* 尖叫声，惊叫声；拼命的叫喊声

例 Women were screaming; some of the houses nearest the bridge were on fire.
女人们在尖叫；离桥最近的几所房屋起火了。

candlelit ['kændllɪt] *adj.* （房间、饭桌）点蜡烛的，用烛光照明的

例 He still finds time for romance by cooking candlelit dinners for his girlfriend.
他仍然会找时间为女友准备烛光晚餐，制造浪漫。

outlive [ˌaʊtˈlɪv] *v.* 比……长寿；度过……而健在

例 The UN is an organization which has long since outlived its usefulness.
联合国是一个早已形同虚设的机构。

singles ['sɪŋgə] *n.* 单程票（single的名词复数）；（旅馆等的）单人房间；未婚（或单身）男子（或女子）*v.* 挑选（single的第三人称单数）

例 The collection includes all the band's British and American hit singles.

专辑中收录了该乐队在英国和美国的所有热门单曲。

unwed [ʌn'wed] *adj.* 没有结婚的，未婚的

例 Nearly one out of three births in America is to an unwed mother.

在美国，几乎每三个新生儿当中就有一个系未婚妈妈所生。

patron ['peɪtrən] *n.* 赞助人，资助人；顾客，老主顾；保护人；[宗]守护神

例 Catherine the Great was a patron of arts and sciences.

叶卡捷琳娜大帝赞助过各种艺术创作和科学研究。

saint [seɪnt] *n.* 圣徒；圣人般的人（指特别善良、仁爱或有耐性的人）

例 Every parish was named after a saint.

每个教区都以某位圣徒的名字命名。

deliberate [dɪ'lɪbərɪt] *adj.* 深思熟虑的；故意的；蓄意的；慎重的 *v.* 权衡；熟虑；商讨

例 It has a deliberate policy to introduce world art to Britain.

它在政策上有意识地将世界艺术介绍给英国。

midlife [mɪd'laɪf] *n.* 中年

例 I went through my midlife crisis about four or five years ago, when I was forty.

四五年前，在我四十岁的时候，我经历了中年危机。

shackle ['ʃækəl] *n.* 束缚；手铐，脚镣；[机]钩环；[电]绝缘器 *v.* 束缚，加枷锁；妨碍，阻碍；给……上手铐；[电]在……装绝缘器

例 The trade unions are shackled by the law.

工会受法律的制约。

patronize ['peɪtrənaɪz] *v.* 惠顾；资助；屈尊；保护

例 Don't you patronize me!

别在我面前摆出一副屈尊俯就的样子！

baggage ['bægɪdʒ] *n.* 行李；辎重；精神包袱

例 The passengers went through immigration control and collected their baggage.

旅客通过入境检查后领取了自己的行李。

语法知识点 *Grammar Points*

① She was close to 50 before she realized the necessity to change jobs and priorities.

这个句子中有两个结构"be close to"和"the necessity to do"，分别表示"接近，离……近"和"干某事的必要性"。后者同义词组还有be necessary to do sth.。

例 The ship kept close to the coast.
那条船靠近海岸航行。

We should bethink ourselves of the necessity to raise more funds.
我们必须考虑到筹集更多基金的必要性。

② She has resolved to break up with this company.

这个句子中有一个结构"resolve to do"，表示"决心做某事"。相当于be determined to do sth.。

例 I resolve to give my customers some control.
我决心给用户一些控制权。

③ ...am I destined to always work hard with "No Life"?

这个句子中有一个结构"be destined to do"，表示"注定会干某事"。相当于be to do或者是be doomed to do。

例 What if I'm destined to fail?
如果我注定要失败怎么办？

④ ...we long for love, we are terribly afraid of dying destitute.

这个句子中有两个结构"long for"和"be afraid of doing"，分别表示"渴望，向往"和"害怕干某事"。

例 Most of all, they long for an emotional connection.
最重要的是，她们渴望感情上的共鸣。

Most people prefer the back because they're afraid of being noticed.
大多数的人们宁愿坐在后面是因为他们害怕被注意。

⑤ **I do not feel like dating at times, just simply because I am not interested in dating or being in a romantic relationship with bald guys unless I meet someone really interesting.**

这个句子中有两个结构 "feel like doing sth." 和 "be interested in"，分别表示"想做某事"和"对……感兴趣"。前者相当于want to do sth.，后者相当于be fond of。

例 I feel like vomitting.
我觉得想呕吐。

But I was interested in another definition of technology.
但我却对科技的另一个定义感兴趣。

经典名句 *Famous Classics*

1. Love with tears is the most moving.
   拌着眼泪的爱情是最动人的。

2. Every noble work is at first impossible.
   每一个伟大的工程最初看起来都是不可能做到的！

3. The shortest way to do many things is to do only one thing at a time.
   做许多事情的捷径就是一次只做一件事。

4. Wasting time is robbing oneself.
   浪费时间就是掠夺自己。

5. If you would know the value of money, go and try to borrow some.
   要想知道钱的价值，就想办法去借钱试试。

读书笔记

30 Unconditional Love
无条件的爱

The following story **took place** long ago in Israel. One day when government officials were rebuilding a **barn**, they found a mouse hole in a corner and used smoke to force the mice inside the hole to come out. A while later they indeed saw mice running out, one after another.

Then, everyone thought that all the mice had **escaped**. But just as they just about to start to **clean up**, they saw two mice **squeezing out** at the exit of the hole. After some **endeavor**, the mice finally got out. The strange thing was that after they came out of the hole, they did not run away immediately. Instead, one chased after the other near the exit of the hole. It seemed that one was trying to bite the tail of the other.

Everyone was **puzzled**, so they stepped closer to take a look. They realized that one of the mice was blind and could not see anything, and the other one was trying to allow the blind mouse to bite on his tail so he could pull the blind one with him to escape.

After **witnessing** what happened, everyone was **speechless** and **lost in thought**. During meal time, the group of

很久以前，在以色列发生了以下一段故事：有一天，政府人员在翻新谷仓时，发现墙角有一个老鼠洞，于是众人用烟熏的方式，希望逼使里面的老鼠出来。过了一会儿，果然看到老鼠一只只地逃窜出来。

众人正忖度老鼠大概已经逃光了，可以上前打扫之际，却见还有两只老鼠在洞口处推挤，经过一番努力，才双双逃出来。但很奇怪的是，两只老鼠出了洞口以后，却不立即逃走，而是在洞口附近互相追赶，像是要咬对方的尾巴似的。

众人都很纳闷，便走上前去细看，这才发现原来其中一只老鼠瞎眼看不见，而另一只正设法使对方咬着自己的尾巴，然后带领同伴一起逃走。

众人见状，都默然不语，陷入沉思中。吃饭的时候，众人又围着坐下，并开始讨论刚才的两只老鼠。

严肃的罗马官员说："我认为刚才的两只老鼠是君臣主仆的关系。"众人思考一会儿后说："原来如此！"于是罗

people sat down in a circle and started to chat about what happened to the two mice.

One serious Rome official said: "I think the relationship between those two mice was that of **emperor** and **minister**." The others thought for a while and said: "That was why!" Thus the Rome official showed his arrogance superciliously.

A smart Israeli said: "I think the relationship between those two mice was husband and wife." Again the others thought for a while, and all felt it made sense; so they expressed assent. Therefore, the Israeli's countenance showed self-satisfaction.

At that moment, one pure-minded Samaritan who was squatted on the ground resting his chin in his palms, **bewilderedly** looked at other people, and asked: "Why did those two mice have to have a certain relationship?"

Suddenly, the **atmosphere** froze. Stupefied, the group looked back at the Samaritan and remained speechless. The Rome official and the Israeli who had spoken earlier all lowered their heads in **shame**, and did not dare to respond.

In fact, the true love is not established on benefit, friendship and loyalty or blood relationship. Instead, it is based on no relationship.

马官兵摆出一副高傲的姿态。

聪明的以色列人说："我认为刚才的两只老鼠是夫妇关系。"众人又思考了一会儿，觉得不错，连声称是。于是以色列人露出一副飘飘然得意的嘴脸。

此时，单纯的撒玛利亚人蹲在地上托着下巴，呆呆地望着众人，问道："为什么那两只老鼠一定要有什么关系呢？"

空气在刹那之间凝固了。众人呆呆地望着这个撒玛利亚人，不发一语。先前说话的罗马官员、以色列人都面露惭色地低下头不敢作声。

事实上，真正的爱并非建基于利益、情义或血缘的关系上，而是建基于"没有任何关系"上。

单词解析 *Word Analysis*

take place 发生，举行

例 A total solar eclipse is due to take place some time tomorrow.
明天某个时刻会发生日全食。

barn [bɑ:rn] *n.* 牲口棚；谷仓，粮仓；（公共汽车、卡车等的）车库

例 He and Walker patched the barn roof.
他和沃克补好了谷仓顶。

escape [ɪ'skeɪp] *v.* 逃脱；逃离；躲过；泄露 *n.* 逃走；逃跑工具或方法；泄漏 *adj.* 使逃避困难的；使规避问题的

例 A prisoner has escaped from a jail in northern England.
一名囚犯从英格兰北部的一所监狱中越狱。

clean up 打扫；<口>赚钱；整顿；痛打

例 Police in the city have been cleaning up the debris left by a day of violent confrontation.
该市警察一直在清理一天的暴力冲突后留下的碎石残砖。

squeeze out 挤出；排挤；榨出；轧

例 Other directors appear to be happy that Lord Hollick has been squeezed out.
其他董事都因为霍利克勋爵被挤了出去而显得很高兴。

endeavor [ɪn'devə] *v.* 尝试，试图；尽力，竭力 *n.* 努力，尽力

例 We made an earnest endeavor to persuade her.
我们郑重其事地努力说服她。

puzzled ['pʌzəld] *adj.* 困惑的，糊涂的，茫然的 *v.*（puzzle的过去式）使迷惑，使难解 *n.* 谜，难题

例 Critics remain puzzled by the British election results.
批评家仍然对英国大选的结果困惑不解。

witness ['wɪtnɪs] *n.* 目击者，见证人；[法]证人；证据 *v.* 目击，目睹；见证，经历

例 Witnesses to the crash say they saw an explosion just before the

disaster.
空难目击者称，就在灾难发生之前他们看见飞机发生了爆炸。

speechless ['spitʃlɪs] *adj.* 无言以对；无言的；（因惊愕）一时语塞的

例 The little boy was speechless with shock.
那小男孩惊得说不出话来。

lost in thought 陷入沉思

例 He sat there, lost in thought.
他坐在那里出神。

emperor ['empərə(r)] *n.* 皇帝，君主

例 In keeping with tradition, the Emperor and Empress did not attend the ceremony.
按照传统，皇帝和皇后未参加该仪式。

minister ['mɪnɪstə] *n.* 部长；大臣；牧师；公使 *v.* 辅助，服侍；执行牧师职务

例 When the government had come to power, he had been named minister of culture.
这届政府开始执政的时候，他被任命为文化部部长。

bewilder [bɪ'wɪldə] *v.* 使迷惑；使为难；使手足无措；使变糊涂

例 So many questions bewilder me.
这样多的问题使我困惑。

atmosphere ['ætməsfɪə] *n.* 气氛；大气层；大气，空气；风格，基调

例 *The Partial Test-Ban Treaty* bans nuclear testing in the atmosphere.
《部分禁止核试验条约》禁止在大气层中进行核试验。

shame [ʃeɪm] *n.* 羞愧；羞辱；可耻的人；羞愧感 *v.* 使蒙羞；玷辱；使感到羞愧；使相形见绌

例 She felt a deep sense of shame.
她深感羞愧。

语法知识点 *Grammar Points*

① The following story took place long ago in Israel.

这个句子中有一个结构 "take place"，表示"发生"。相当于 come off 和 happen。

例 When does the wedding take place?
什么时候举行婚礼？

② But just as they just about to start to clean up, they saw two mice squeezing out at the exit of the hole.

这个句子中有一个结构 "squeeze out"，相当于"挤出，榨出，排出"。

例 Hearing that, she tried to squeeze out a smile.
听到这话，她挤出一丝微笑。

③ Everyone was puzzled, so they stepped closer to take a look.

这句话中有一个结构 "take a look"，表示"看一下"。相当于 have a look 或者 look，同样用法的动词还有 take a rest 和 rest，take a walk 和 walk 等。

例 Should I take a look at your battery?
要我帮您看一下电池吗？

④ They realized that one of the mice was blind and could not see anything, and the other one was trying to allow the blind mouse to bite on his tail so he could pull the blind one with him to escape.

这句话中有两个结构 "one of" 和 "one...the other..."，分别表示"其中一个"和"一个……另一个……"。one of 后面用名词复数。

例 English poetry is one of their great heritages.
英国诗歌是他们的伟大遗产之一。

⑤ The Rome official and the Israeli who had spoken earlier all lowered their heads in shame, and did not dare to respond.

这个句子中有一个结构 "in shame" 和 "dare to do"，分别表示"羞耻地"和"敢于干某事"。

例 She hung her head in shame.
她羞愧地低下头。

If the enemy dare to invade us, we'll deal them head-on blows.
敌人胆敢进犯，我们就给以迎头痛击。

经典名句 *Famous Classics*

1. Even if the whole world leave you, I am here right for you.
   就算全世界离开你，还有一个我来陪。
2. I am in a city, waiting for a friend to come.
   我在一座孤城，等待一个旧人的到来。
3. I'm not afraid of anything, even if I am alone.
   我并不畏惧什么，哪怕我一直都是一个人。
4. I was born for you, and you were there for me.
   我为你而生，你因我而存在。
5. Love can't be measured by common sense.
   爱情不能用常识衡量。

读书笔记

31 Beauty Within
心灵之爱

John Blanchard stood up from the bench, **straightened** his Army uniform, and studied the crowd of people making their way through Grand Central Station.

He was looking for the girl whose heart he knew, but whose face he didn't, the girl with the rose. His interest in her had begun 12 months before in a Florida library. Taking a book off the shelf he found himself absorbed, not by the words of the book, but by the notes penciled in the **margin**. The soft handwriting showed a thoughtful soul and **insightful** mind.

In the front of the book, he discovered the previous owner's name, Miss Hollis Maynell. With time and effort he found her exact address. She lived in New York City. He wrote her a letter introducing himself and inviting her to write him. The next day he was shipped to another country for service in World War II.

During the next year and one month the two grew to know each other through the mail. Each letter was a seed falling on a fertile heart. A love

约翰·布兰查德从长凳上站起身来，整了整军装，留意着格兰德中央车站进出的人群。

他在寻找一位姑娘，一位佩戴玫瑰的姑娘，一位他只知其心，不知其貌的姑娘。十二个月前，在佛罗里达州的一个图书馆里，他对她产生了兴趣。他从书架上取下一本书，很快便被吸引住了，不是被书的内容，而是被空白处铅笔写的批语所吸引。柔和的笔迹显示出其人多思善虑的心灵和富有洞察力的头脑。

在书的前页，他找到了书的前任主人的姓名：霍利斯·梅奈尔小姐。他花了一番工夫，找到了她的确切地址。她住在纽约市。他给她写了一封信介绍自己，并请她回复。第二天他被运送到海外，参加第二次世界大战。

在接下来的一年零一个月中，两人通过信件来往增进了对彼此的了解。每一封信都如一颗种子撒入肥沃的心灵之土。浪漫的爱情之花开始绽开。布兰查德提出要一张照

began to develop. Blanchard requested a **photograph**, but she refused. She explained: "If your feeling for me has any reality, any honest basis, what I look like won't matter. Suppose I'm beautiful I'd always be worried by the feeling that you had been taking a chance on just that, and that kind of love would make me sick. Suppose I'm plain and you must admit that this is more likely. Then I would always fear that you were going on writing to me only because you were lonely and had no one else. No, don't ask for my picture. When you come to New York, you shall see me and then you shall make your own decision. Remember, both of us are free to stop or to go on after that—whichever we choose…"

片，可她拒绝了。她解释道：

"如果你对我的感情是真实的，是诚心诚意的，那我的容貌如何并不重要。设想我美丽动人，我会始终深感不安，唯恐你只是因为我的容貌就贸然与我相爱，而这种爱情令我厌恶。设想本人相貌平平（你得承认，这种可能性更大），那我就会始终担心，你和我保持通信仅仅是出于孤独寂寞，无人交谈。不，别索要照片。等你到了纽约，你会见到我，到时你可再做定夺。切记，见面后我俩都可以自由决定中止关系或继续交往——无论你我怎么选择……"

单词解析 *Word Analysis*

straighten ['streʃn] Ⓥ 变直，把……弄直；整理，整顿；使……改正；使……好转

例 She sipped her coffee and straightened a picture on the wall.
她抿了口咖啡，然后把墙上的一幅画扶正。

margin ['mɑːrdʒən] Ⓝ 边缘，范围；极限；利润，盈余；（版心外）的空白

例 She added her comments in the margin.
她在页边的空白处写下了评语。

insightful ['ɪn,saɪtfəl,ɪn'saɪt-] *adj.* 富有洞察力的，有深刻见解的

例 This is a more insightful definition than you might think.

这是比你所想到的更为深刻的定义。

photograph ['foʊtəgræf] *n.* 照片，相片 *v.* 为……拍照；拍照，摄影；成为拍照对象

例 He wants to take some photographs of the house.
他想给这幢房子拍一些照片。

fertile ['fɜːrtl] *adj.* 肥沃的；可繁殖的；想象力丰富的

例 A chess player must have a fertile imagination and rich sense of fantasy.
一个棋手必须有丰富的想象力，并善于奇思妙想。

admit [æd'mɪt] *v.* 许可进入；承认，供认；允许；确认

例 I am willing to admit that I do make mistakes.
我愿意承认我确实会犯错。

语法知识点 *Grammar Points*

① **He looked for the girl whose heart he knew, but whose face he didn't, the girl with the rose.**

这个句子中有一个结构 "look for"，表示 "寻找"。Look for 和 find 不同，前者是寻找的过程，后者是寻找的结果。

例 He looked for his dog for a whole day but failed to find it.
他找他的狗找了一天，但是并未找到。

② **He wrote her a letter introducing himself and inviting her to write him.**

这个句子中有一个结构 "invite sb. to do sth."，表示 "邀请某人做某事"。

例 My father and mother want to invite you to go to the movies.
我父母想邀请你一起去看电影。

③ **During the next year and one month the two grew to know each other through the mail.**

这个句子中有一个结构 "grow to do sth."，表示 "逐渐开始做某事"。相当于 gradually begin to do。

例 She grew to know how to do this.
她慢慢开始知道如何做了。

④ **Suppose I'm beautiful I'd always be worried by the feeling that you had been taking a chance on just that, and that kind of love would make me sick.**

这个句子中有一个结构"take a chance"，表示"抓住机会，冒险一试"。suppose是指假设……结果会如何，相当于 if。

例 He decided to take a chance.
他决定冒险一试。

⑤ **Remember, both of us are free to stop or to go on after that——whichever we choose…**

这个句子中有一个结构"be free to do"，表示"有自由干某事"。相当于 have freedom to do。

例 I am free to do what I want.
我可以自由地做我想做的事。

经典名句 *Famous Classics*

1. Sow nothing, reap nothing.
春不播，秋不收。

2. Keep on going and never give up.
勇往直前，决不放弃！

3. The wealth of the mind is the only wealth.
精神的财富是唯一的财富。

4. Never say die.
永不气馁！

5. Nurture passes nature.
教养胜过天性。

32 The Warm of a Cup of Milk
一杯牛奶的温暖

One day, a poor boy who was trying to pay his way through school by selling goods door to door found that he only had one dime left. He was hungry so he decided to beg for a meal at the next house.

However, he lost his nerve when a lovely young woman opened the door. Instead of a meal he asked for a drink of water. She thought he looked hungry so she brought him a large glass of milk. He drank it slowly, and then asked, "How much do I **owe** you?"

"You don't owe me anything." she replied, "Mother has taught me never to accept pay for a kindness." He said, "Then I thank you from the bottom of my heart." As Howard Kelly left that house, he not only felt stronger physically, but it also increased his **faith** in God and the human race. He was about to give up and quit before this point.

Years later the young woman became critically ill. The local doctors were **baffled**. They finally sent her to the big city, where specialists can be called in to study her **rare disease**. Dr. Howard Kelly, now famous was

一天，一个贫穷的小男孩为了攒够学费正在挨家挨户地推销商品。饥寒交迫的他摸遍全身，却只有一枚一角硬币。于是他决定向下一户人家讨口饭吃。

然而，当一位美丽的年轻女子打开房门的时候，这个小男孩却有点不知所措了。他没有要饭，只乞求给他一口水喝。这位女子看到他饥饿的样子，就倒了一大杯牛奶给他。男孩慢慢地喝完牛奶，问道："我要付你多少钱？"

年轻女子微笑着回答："一分钱也不用付。我妈妈教导我，施以爱心，不求回报。"男孩说："那么，就请接受我由衷的感谢吧！"说完，霍华德·凯利就离开了这户人家。此时的他不仅浑身是劲儿，而且更加相信上帝和整个人类。本来他都打算放弃了。

数年之后，那位女子得了一种罕见的重病，当地医生都对此束手无策。最后，她转到大医院医治，由专家会诊治疗。大名鼎鼎的霍华德·凯

called in for the consultation. When he heard the name of the town she came from, a strange light filled his eyes. Immediately, he rose and went down through the hospital hall into her room.

Dressed in his doctor's gown he went in to see her. He recognized her at once. He went back to the consultation room and determined to do his best to save her life. From that day on, he gave special attention to her case.

After a long struggle, the battle was won. Dr. Kelly **requested** the business office to pass the final bill to him for approval. He looked at it and then wrote something on the side. The bill was sent to her room. She was afraid to open it because she was positive that it would take the rest of her life to pay it off. Finally she looked, and the note on the side of the bill caught her attention. She read these words…

"Paid in full with a glass of milk."

(Signed) Dr. Howard Kelly

Tears of joy flooded her eyes as she prayed silently: "Thank You, God. Your love has spread through human hearts and hands."

利医生也参加了医疗方案的制定。当他听到病人来自的那个城镇的名字时，一个奇怪的念头霎时闪过他的脑际。他马上起身直奔她的病房。

身穿手术服的凯利医生来到病房，一眼就认出了恩人。回到会诊室后，他决心一定要竭尽所能来治好她的病。从那天起，他就特别关照这个对自己有恩的病人。

经过艰苦的努力，手术成功了。凯利医生要求把医药费通知单送到他那里，他看了一下，便在通知单的旁边签了字。当医药费通知单送到那个女子病房时，她不敢看。因为她确信，治病的费用将会花费她整个余生来偿还。最后，她还是鼓起勇气，翻开了医药费通知单，旁边的那行小字引起了她的注意，她不禁轻声读了出来：

"医药费已付：一杯牛奶。"

（签名）霍华德·凯利医生

幸福的眼泪涌出她的眼眶，同时，她默默地祈祷："感谢您，上帝。您的爱已经洒遍了人们的心灵和双手。"

单词解析 *Word Analysis*

owe [əʊ] *v.* 欠；感激；应给予；应该把……归功于

例 I owe him nothing.
我不欠他什么。

faith [feɪθ] *n.* 忠诚；信用，信任；宗教信仰；宗教 *int.* 实在，确实

例 She had placed a great deal of faith in Mr Penleigh.
她对彭利先生极其信任。

baffle ['bæfəl] *v.* 使受挫折；使困惑，使迷惑；用隔音板隔音；挡住（水流等）*n.* 隔板，挡板；迷惑；遮护物，阻碍体；[军]迷彩

例 An apple tree producing square fruit is baffling experts.
一棵结方形苹果的树令专家大惑不解。

rare disease 罕见病

例 She got a rare disease since she went to Africa.
自从她去了非洲后就染上了一种罕见的疾病。

request [rɪ'kwest] *n.* 请求；需要 *v.* 要求，请求

例 We did it at her request.
我们应她的要求而做。

语法知识点 *Grammar Points*

① **One day, a poor boy who was trying to pay his way through school by selling goods door to door found that he only had one dime left.**

这句话中有一个结构 "try to do"，表示 "努力做某事"。相当于try one's best to和do one's utmost to。

例 But I try to be close to her.
但是我会努力站在她身边。

② **He was hungry so he decided to beg for a meal at the next house.**

这句话中有两个结构 "decide to do" 和 "beg for"，分别表示 "决定干某事" 和 "乞讨，乞求"。

例 It all depends on what you decide to believe.
这一切都取决于你决定要相信什么。

Those words bring nothing but pain and yet we beg for it.
这些话除了伤痛什么也不能带来，而我们却还乞求它。

③ **Instead of a meal he asked for a drink of water.**

这句话中有一个结构"instead of"，表示"代替，而不是"。

例 Instead of abating, the wind is blowing even harder.
风不但没停，反而越刮越大了。

④ **He was about to give up and quit before this point.**

这句话中有两个结构"be about to do"和"give up"，分别表示"即将，正要干某事"和"放弃"。前者相当于be going to；后者相当于quit。

例 She was about to speak when she was stopped by her sister.
她刚要说话，被她姐姐拦住了。

They refused to give up.
他们拒绝放弃。

⑤ **He went back to the consultation room and determined to do his best to save her life. From that day on, he gave special attention to her case.**

这句话中有两个结构"determine to do"和"do one's best to"，分别表示"决定干某事"和"尽力做某事"。

例 He determined to rescue his two countrymen.
他决定要救两个同胞。

One should do one's best to serve the people.
人人都应尽最大努力为人民服务。

⑥ **She was afraid to open it because she was positive that it would take the rest of her life to pay it off.**

这句话中有一个结构"be afraid to do"，表示"害怕做某事"。相当于be scared/frightened to do sth.。

例 The shy girl was afraid to contradict.
这个害羞的女孩不敢提出反驳意见。

经典名句 *Famous Classics*

1. Love you for all my life.
   爱你一辈子。

2. The way to do the work is to cherish every minute.
   完成工作的方法是爱惜每一分钟。

3. It made me look like a duck in water.
   它让我如鱼得水。

4. I don't know if we each have a destiny, or if we're all just floating around accidentally—like on a breeze.
   我不知道我们能否有着各自的运气，还是只是随风飘荡。

5. Everything you see exists together in a delicate balance.
   世界上全部的生命都在微妙的平衡中生活。

读书笔记

读书笔记